Healthcare Leadership in Times of Crisis

Dennis W. Tafoya · Lindsey Poeth

Healthcare Leadership in Times of Crisis

A Model for Managing Threats to Organizations

Dennis W. Tafoya
CompCite
Devon, PA, USA

Lindsey Poeth
Oasis Senior Advisors
Malvern, PA, USA

ISBN 978-3-030-75964-3   ISBN 978-3-030-75965-0   (eBook)
https://doi.org/10.1007/978-3-030-75965-0

This Palgrave Macmillan imprint is published by the registered company Springer Nature Switzerland AG
The registered company address is: Gewerbestrasse 11, 6330 Cham, Switzerland

This book is dedicated to the employees of healthcare organizations who demonstrate the competencies needed to adapt to changing situations. They are the doctors, nurses, technicians and emergency medical technicians associated with healthcare delivery and the all-important support services that feed, clean and repair equipment and operations so that health delivery is possible.

Preface

The material in this book bundles together two components of organizational theory: One that reflects the successful operation of an organization and the other that defines the nature of organizational leadership required when facing dangerous or troublesome events. It differs from most treatments of these two areas because challenging events or emerging crises require leadership of a different sort. This is the leadership that adds to the management of day-to-day operations of a functioning organization to include leadership that may, in the extreme, be expected to lead the organization's stakeholders.

Through the research efforts associated with this book, we saw numerous illustrations of healthcare professionals who augmented their management or regular duties to lead change efforts. Their actions were not defined by the nature of their jobs or positions but by the needs for change they experienced. Collectively, their actions reflected three behaviors we believe are needed when managing a problem event or emerging crisis. These are the immediate first elements of leadership and they are described as follows:

First, "Vision". This is not vision in the typical sense one expects to see in a problem-solving situation but the vision to see and measure the relationship between an event and the organization's mission. Vision of this type requires understanding of the organization's stream of activities, products and services to meet the needs of stakeholders within the organization's social network. This is a critical leadership characteristic because vision in this regard is fundamental to the protection of the organization's overall alignment as an institution.

Second, "Competency". Here again, we did not see competency limited to the personal competency associated with one's professional areas, but rather leadership competencies that reflected the capacity to influence and utilize resources available throughout the organization's social network. At this level, these professionals demonstrated leadership competencies needed to influence and utilize the organization's social network as a solution-producing entity.

Third, Not just Action but Action Committed to Change. Clearly, anyone faced with a challenging, threatening, troublesome event or emerging crisis knows that some change is necessary to avoid pain or loss. But the "Change Leadership" we saw demonstrated led action responses in three important ways.

First there was little hesitation but rather immediate action aimed at anticipating real and potential needs associated with a troublesome event. Competency and vision both played a role in behaviors at this level. These leaders did not wait for information or ideas to emerge, they sought the material and perspectives needed for action.

Second, leadership in this instance took action to address the troublesome event as it emerged. Communication and cognition drive the anticipation of needs to address real or potential threats. Actually taking action is the construction of behavior aimed at change. The medical metaphor for action at this level is described as "triage"; it is the sorting of and allocation of treatment resources to block, redirect or otherwise address the threat at hand. Triage is a familiar concept among medical professionals but "leadership triage" is action aimed at addressing potentially systemic needs of the organization and its social network. It truly is a composite competency.

Finally, in many ways the action taken also reflected an orientation to change driven as much by the future as by the present. At the immediate level the event is managed or the crisis is contained. Leadership with a eye to the future, to the period after the event is managed or a crisis is contained. It is guidance that seeks to treat everything associated with the event or crisis as material resources, potentially capable of defining a new, more responsive future organization.

Dr. Marschall Runge, M.D., Ph.D. and Dean of the University of Michigan's Medical School described what leadership at this level looks like in recent blogs and emails.[1] It is a long summary but it seems an appropriate way to end this introduction while pointing to the book's ultimate objectives: to help leaders see that returning to the way things were is never acceptable if at all possible and that learning from any troublesome event or crisis is possible if leaders lead as they should.

Dr. Runge's observation illustrate leadership of the type we are seeking. He wrote the following:

Our difficult journey over the last two months has presented a clear view of our opportunities and our shortcomings, and we believe we can learn from those in order to make sustained changes that will improve healthcare for all. Now is the time for us to look to the future and create what will become our new normal.

What has COVID-19 taught us?

First and foremost, **we must build a stronger system** that will be better prepared to weather any future crisis. While the quality of care and the intensity, commitment and compassion throughout Michigan Medicine has been unparalleled, we can further improve on our performance should another crisis arise. This will become important as soon as a few months from now if we see an anticipated second wave of COVID-19 cases. Our ability to rapidly establish a regional infection containment unit, or RICU, is just one great example of how we met this challenge at the onset of the COVID-19 crisis.

To continue to lead in this industry, we must become **more productive and efficient**, adapt even more quickly to new technologies and anticipate the needs of our patients, their families, our staff and our communities. Indeed, we have already started great work that will be vital for our future. Here are just a few examples:

- The pandemic forced us to think and act with thoughtful, non-negotiable urgency. This culminated in our command center, which brought a cross-functional team of leaders together to discuss, strategize and make decisions on critical issues. This **daily collaboration** will continue as a part of our new normal.
- Shelter-in-place requirements drove us to utilize a variety of technologies to connect with each other and to reach out to our patients and their families. We have proven that with tools like Zoom, many in our work force can do their jobs **remotely**, while still being effective and productive.
- From a clinical perspective, we are setting new paradigms for provider and patient interactions. In the month of March, we conducted over 8000 virtual visits, which is a far greater number than we achieved over the prior year. We will continue virtual visits as a first-line option, which will greatly **improve access**. The vast majority of our patients (and providers) who used virtual health grew to like it for its convenience and ready access.
- Based on what we learned about our hospital and clinical capacity through the pandemic, we know we need to move forward with **24/7 hospital operations and 12/7** clinic hours in order to reduce length of stay, minimize disruptions in care and standardize practices across our departments and units.
- Although some research came to a halt at many of our labs, our **researchers** turned to technology-driven solutions to continue their work. The COVID-19 research that began during the past two months, as well as their regular research, will continue.

It will be a challenging journey for Michigan Medicine to establish the many "new normals" that will best meet the changing healthcare needs of our communities, and also a long journey for us to recover from the losses and financial impacts of this pandemic.

Devon, USA   Dennis W. Tafoya
Malvern, USA   Lindsey Poeth

Note

1. Runge, Marschall S., M.D., Ph.D. "A New Normal at Michigan Medicine", Friday 01/05/20 2:59 PM.

Acknowledgments

We have had many conversations with healthcare professionals across a variety of areas, too many to recognize individually. But we can acknowledge the particular and ongoing contribution of our friend and colleague Dr. Nancy A. Gripshover. Nancy's thoughts and efforts made this book a truly useful tool for our readers. We cannot thank her enough for her efforts and contributions.

We also want to recognize our editor at Palgrave, Marcus Ballenger. Marcus is a truly adept enabler. He provides candid assessments of our work, is particularly adept at finding and matching the best reviewers for our project. He is a writer's advocate and an apt leader throughout the publishing process where he always demonstrates unparalleled problem-solving skills and competencies.

Contents

List of Figures

List of Tables

1

The Book's Scope and Approach

Abstract Managing any organization on a day-to-day basis can present an array of challenges for anyone with leadership responsibilities. However, when faced with a traumatic event or crisis there are two particularly unique challenges that can add layers of difficulty to the task at hand. The first of these is that because the various parts of an organization are linked in some manner, a crisis, by its nature, will likely effect many areas of the organization and its stakeholders in numerous and diverse ways. The second issue, equally challenging, is one of an especially personal nature for an organization's leadership. In many instances, an individual's competencies define the capacity to lead a crisis containment effort. Leadership in these instances affects the capacity to manage changing conditions, to affect individual behavior and, the ability to influence the thinking and behavior of others within the wider social network.

Keywords Events · Crises · Catastrophes · Disasters

D. W. Tafoya and L. Poeth, *Healthcare Leadership in Times of Crisis*,
https://doi.org/10.1007/978-3-030-75965-0_1

1

Managing an organization on a day-to-day basis can present an array of challenges for anyone with leadership responsibilities. However, when faced with a traumatic event or crisis, there are two particularly unique challenges that can add layers of difficulty to the task at hand. The first of these is that because the various parts of an organization are linked in some manner, a crisis, by its nature, will likely effect many areas of the organization and its stakeholders in numerous and diverse ways.

Injuries, broken processes, delays and general confusion are only some of the spin-off effects to manage in a crisis containment effort. Disorganization may rule if staff are surprised or caught off guard when a crisis emerges. Lack of organization or poorly defined routines may add different threats, risks and vulnerabilities to an already troublesome situation.

The second issue, equally challenging, is one of an especially personal nature for an organization's leadership. In many instances, an individual's competencies define the capacity to lead a crisis containment effort. Leadership in these instances affects the capacity to manage changing conditions, to affect individual behavior and actions and, the ability to influence the thinking and behavior of others outside of the immediate organization; members of the organization's wider stakeholder network.

To gain insight into how these two factors can affect efforts to contain a crisis consider the Table 1.1. Crises are always disruptive; they established disrupt routines, the communication and information flows among stakeholders and, as a crisis progresses to a catastrophe or disastrous state, the organization's very risks, threats and vulnerabilities. These are destabilizing changes with immediate and, if uncontrolled, long-term effects.

But crises also present conditions which can challenge an individual's social and professional capacity to respond and lead in efforts to contain the crisis. As Table 1.1 illustrates, each of the four states, from event through the maturation of a disaster, present new and potentially unique tests for those involved. The following chapters cover material that tracks ways in which a mismanaged event can trigger a crisis, catastrophe or disaster. These chapters build off research and discussions to map how these phenomena produce effects that ripple through the organization

Table 1.1 Progressive contamination and distress: Change dominates leadership decisions making

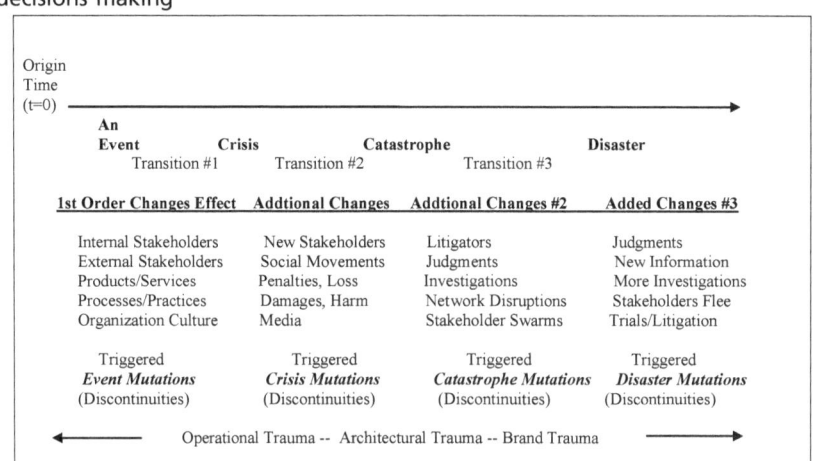

and its social networks. In the end people, processes, products, services and, relationships are affected.

The healthcare organizations provide a unique opportunity for illustrating the material and claims associated with the book's major themes. Recent experience with the coronavirus phenomenon among organizations in these industries is an excellent point of departure for this discussion. Using our models, the emergence of the virus provided an example of an event that needed immediate and specific management. However, management responses and, in some cases early mismanagement, triggered the crises that emerged to encumber healthcare systems and personnel in and outside these organizations.

Some healthcare systems folded under the pressures triggered by the virus' effects. In other instances, fear of facilitating the virus' spread contributed to the suspension of some healthcare delivery processes. A hospital's elective surgeries were postponed. Satellite areas like dentistry, those associated with eye care or even physical therapy that other organizations like nursing homes and eldercare communities rely on had operations restricted, sometimes suspended.[1] Finally, as the virus grew in magnitude and more was learned about ways specific populations were affected, healthcare agencies that addressed the needs of the elderly remained in operation but were often closed to all but existing residents. The result: what was an otherwise vibrant, highly integrated health-care system, with multiple inter-dependencies became a collection of often standalone treatment centers with a two-fold objective: treat those infected with the virus and protect those within the organization's care, custody and control from exposure to the virus.

The Idea of a "New Normal" Is a Misnomer

When organizations slip into a crisis' grip, familiar operations can end as people learn to refer to the "new normal" defining their current way of life. This phrase is a way to describe a period of "constrained fluidity"; a period where operations continued, but not in ways that were earlier described as "business as usual." But what is the new normal, if nothing more than a period of continuous adjustment, amendment or, alteration of previously familiar practices and procedures? And, importantly, in what ways does the emergence of a traumatic event and subsequent crisis influence the daily activities in healthcare organizations?

Material that follows is written to address these and related questions. In the book healthcare delivery is addressed by looking at the dynamics within and among key providers and, by extension, the many ancillary organizations uniquely linked in support relationships. This review is unique because while independent, standalone organizations with their own client bases seem capable of managing events and crises that emerge, things change when the threats are unusually significant and affect a number of organizations in and outside the immediate network. In these instances, the very healthcare delivery processes developed and nurtured over time become vulnerable because of the co-dependent relationships shared with others. Individual business models become complicated as the systemic nature of these co-dependencies reveal that in a pandemic such as COVID-19 it is not one or two stakeholders that are distressed, but many or even most in the overall network.

When a crisis emerges all relationships in the intricate healthcare stakeholder network are affected. Consider a fire in a nursing home. Regardless of the size, nature or location of the fire, first attention must focus on residents. Many may have existing destabilizing medical conditions, but now the emergence of a fire event means that spreading smoke, flames and heat from the fire and, a potentially growing sense of terror among incapacitated residents means other actions must be taken. Safe areas outside the facility must be identified and evacuation to those safe areas must begin. Ambulances summoned as a precaution or to ferry the injured to a hospital can fill driveways and complicate traffic patterns while hospital emergency departments are notified, and medical staff called in and put on notice. And, while all of this "change" is occurring, someone has to think about the arriving fire trucks, police, media vehicles and family cars on their way to be someway involved in the original event—the fire.

This fire event is a simple illustration on one level but, given the nature of the nursing home and eldercare communities this simple illustration reveals the manner in which even a "simple" event can trigger a cascade of phenomena capable of stressing and traumatizing an otherwise stable social network. Clearly, recent experience with the coronavirus is a timely example of the types of events and subsequent crises that healthcare organizations must manage and/or contain. But the coronavirus, while a significant event, is just an example for us and our research.

Nursing homes and other healthcare facilities are peppered with daily events, any one of which could trigger a crisis of debilitating nature. There is the potential for loss of life in a healthcare environment or the spread of pathogens in treatment areas. Labor issues are topics of concern for all healthcare organizations as competitive pressures, economic conditions or legal requirements for operational practices continue to define the operating environments for these firms. Yet these are just the "common" occurrences. We have not yet mentioned charges of elder abuse, careless or neglect in treatment protocols or, even the notion that an organization's overall environment creates hostile or threatening atmospheres for its patients or residents—whatever that means![2]

Everything Begins with an Event

Managing events is the critical first step in crisis avoidance but how well events are managed is largely dependent on the effectiveness of an organization's staff and the extent to which they function vis a vis the organization's architecture, processes and brand. Competencies are best demonstrated against a backdrop of a strong and proven architecture. The organization's architecture contributes to stakeholder cohesiveness by keeping information and communication channels open. On a more systemic level the architecture keeps information systems up and running adding to an employee's capacity to perform or, if involved, to help address the event at hand.

Strong and well-maintained processes make real contributions to the overall organizational event management effort. Operational processes focus on achieving a goal. In non-event or non-crisis times the processes are centered on the work to be done, on one's task at hand. When a problem event emerges, established processes become opportunities to transfer time, skills and materials to supplement *processes that are event-specific for the problem event*. For example, processes related to safety or quality can be amended to meet the needs of those attempting to contain the event. New approaches are developed, to be sure, but these often work best if couched in the already known and familiar processes employees use on a daily basis. Finally, an organization's brand helps stakeholders align with the organization's mission and efforts during event management efforts. Belief in the brand can enable buy-into management efforts. Brand affiliation supplements belief or hope that the organization will succeed in addressing the troublesome event in good shape; in many instances, an organization's brand is the first reason why potential patients or clients are willing to consider the organization as a place that can meet their healthcare needs.

When an event emerges the same skills and competencies that allowed the organization's personnel to operate effectively prior to the event may not match those needed to manage this new and challenging situation. In short, competencies, skills and experience needed to contain the crisis and manage its effects may be beyond those the leadership team possesses. Our focus throughout the book examines these and other challenges. On one level we explore ways in which an organization's architecture, operational processes and brand can contribute to the strategies and tactics used for treating events, containing an emerging crisis and managing a crisis' effects. Yet, on another level, we also examine ways in which a mismanaged event and subsequent crisis damages an organization's architecture, processes and brand.

Throughout the book, considerable time is devoted to the personal challenges that emerge for those expected to take a leadership role in crisis containment efforts. This is important for mastering one's competencies must occur in order to bring direct, potential benefits to the task. However, perhaps the greatest benefits associated with maximizing one's competencies are the contributions these make to an individual's capacity to be influential in crisis or non-crisis times. The capacity to be influential is a true leadership characteristic and one that contributes to a range of opportunities for a professional.

Finally, the book explores various challenges in terms of the inherent nature of organizations in the healthcare industry. While organizations comprising this industry can serve the same populations they operate under different models. Different rules and regulations, missions, practices and procedures and professional staffing requirements define them, which makes a crisis' impact on them of particular interest. In many ways when a crisis emerges those exposed to it or associated with its containment are in a unique position: they are in a position to see, in real time, the exposures to threats, risks and vulnerabilities associated with an event vis a vis their own skills and competencies to manage the event.

Classroom instruction is a way for creating vicarious scenarios for the student. It is a way to describe or talk about events that may trigger a crisis. Think about this point, however. Organizations spend thousands of dollars to develop and prepare quality, safety and security programs as pre-emptive strategies for "things that might happen." Those participating take their leadership's suggestion regarding the value of these programs in good faith. However, a problem with pre-emptive strategies is that over time complacency may compromise any sense of urgency behind the need for programs and training.

Thick books outlining the pre-emptive programs are shelved and seldom looked at or revised. Tools and materials like "material safety data sheets" are misplaced, or with the often unused fire extinguisher, allowed to "go flat" and useless. Worse, sometimes even training associated with these programs is viewed as a "bother" or, worse, "useless." People dread the fire drills and may try to skip them altogether. Similar conclusions can be drawn regarding department safety training—sometimes even taught by someone unfamiliar with the program or having training skills. A result, when faced with the threatening event panics and fears for self-survival can supplant any sense of urgency demanded by the situation.

We pay special attention to understanding ways in which an emerging crisis can capitalize on the risks, vulnerabilities and exposures inherent in healthcare organizations. In contrast to other organizations, these organizations operate with particular constraints linked to the nature of the organizations and, importantly, their client base. For example, particular laws, rules and regulations define both the nature of hospitals or nursing homes and the ways in which they are permitted to operate as stand-alone entities. Failure to perform within expected legal parameters can disrupt operations or, worse, lead to the termination of operations in extreme instances.

Finally, as in the Case with an Event, Even if You Contain the Emerging Crisis That Doesn't Mean You Are Ready for the Next Thing on the Horizon!

If we have the opportunity to stand back and watch an organization manage a threatening event or to successfully contain a crisis to its end, what is next for the organization? For example, as Table 1.1 illustrates a lot can happen within an organization between the time an event or crisis emerges and it is managed or contained; a lot happens but what long-term "learnings" are taking place? Certainly, people adjust to the event or crisis and react in ways to meet impending needs but, in the end, to what benefit?

We believe that the organization's leadership, from its boards and advisors to its executive and administrative staffs must use events and crises as reasons or even "excuses" for making change in the organization. We say this because one obvious by-product of event management and/or crisis containment is that elements of change have already taken place. Go back to our fire example. Once the residents of the burning nursing home are brought outside to "safety," lots of things are learned. Like, "this isn't the best place for these people given that ambulances and fire trucks are coming," or, "it's rather cold at night, shouldn't we have coats or blankets for these people?" or, "what do we say to media in times like this when they arrive?" So what happens to these "learnings"?

Moreover, reflecting on our observation regarding the convenient use of terms like "a new normal" does that mean that collecting in a parking lot while the fire department is making sure the fire is out and that the building is safe for re-entry will reflect something of the organization's "new normal"? Leadership needed after the event or crisis illustrates that the future may requiere a different set of competencies. How have stakeholders changed with the event or crisis? What about staff? During the early periods of the COVID-19 event, many staff found solutions that worked for them: they simply left or took a "leave of absence" until it will be safe to return.

What about the organization's architecture, processes and brand? What "leadership concerns" have the event or crisis raised for these key organizational features? And, as importantly as all others, what about the organization's stakeholder networks? A crisis pressures both internal and external networks but to what effect and in what ways do the organization's leadership need to respond?

Finally, for all leadership positions involved, from the board and advisors, through the executive and administrative staffs how will success be tested and measured when the real "new normal" evolves? "Just doing" is never enough during or after the event or crisis. Whatever is or has been done must be evaluated using valid and reliable tools. Get ready. They are here!

Notes

1. Englund, Will. "Nursing Homes Say They 'Treat In Place.' Then Came Covid-19. Why Did so Many Nursing Home Residents Die of Covid-19 on site, and Not in Hospitals?" WashingtonPost.com, June 16, 2020 at 11:00 am EDT.
2. Rein, Lisa. "VA Inspector General Exposes Breakdown at D.C. Hospital That Preceded Veteran's Suicide." *The Washington Post*, July 28, 2020 at 3:48 p.m. EDT.

2

The Dynamic Make-up of Healthcare Delivery Threatened by Troublesome Events and/or Crises

Abstract Traumatic events, crises, catastrophes and disasters disrupt an organization's natural order. Disruption occurs in part because of the nature of the phenomena impacting the organization but the scope and scale, sometimes the sheer magnitude of the effects associated with these phenomena, is directly linked to the extent to which the organization exists as a stable, functioning entity. This chapter's material is much like a survey one might use if conducting an audit or review. The premise behind the chapter, is that it is not just an event or how prepared an organization is for the event that makes the biggest difference when an event or crisis emerges. Rather, the biggest factor determining how well the organization and its staff will respond may depend on the extent to which the organization's foundation enables or hinders performance in the face of the event or crisis.

Keywords Performance and performance management · Organizational drivers · Organizational framework

Introduction

Traumatic events, crises, catastrophes and disasters disrupt an organization's natural order. Disruption occurs in part because of the nature of the phenomena impacting the organization, but the scope and scale, sometimes the sheer magnitude of the effects associated with these phenomena, is directly linked to the extent to which the organization exists as a stable, functioning entity. In other words, the extent to which an organization is unmistakably well thought-out, effectively administered or satisfactorily functioning conveys a sense regarding how well it might weather a threatening event or crisis.

In this chapter, features of healthcare organizations provide informal insight into the operational nature of these systems. The chapter's material is much like a survey one might use if conducting an audit or review. The premise behind the chapter, and indeed the entire book, is that it is not just an event or how prepared an organization is for the event that makes the biggest difference when an event or crisis emerges. Rather, the biggest factor determining how well the organization and its staff will respond may depend on the extent to which the organization's foundation enables or hinders performance in the face of the event or crisis. For example, does the event or crisis disrupt the staffs' ability to work toward the organization's vision or mission? Are performance objectives dismissed given the pressing needs brought on by the event or crisis? Is the organization's design compromised so that the capacity to deliver products and services is affected? Are stakeholders inside AND outside the organization unable to articulate ways their participation, support and cooperation are part of a collective effort? Finally, how well does the organization's culture support stakeholder efforts during these trying times? Does the culture nurture, enable and empower or not?

Four Elements Associated with an Organization's Systemic Structural Design

Whether we are observing an organization functioning in day-to-day matters or, in the extreme, when faced with a traumatic event or crisis, the role of four structural elements serves as a benchmark for performance. Diagram 2.1 illustrates these four elements. These structural elements reflect the type of organization, a factor which proves to be an especially interesting factor to consider with crises like the COVID-19 virus. A second element, the organization's structural framework within which those in the organizations function is clearly related to the first, and also one to watch when a troublesome event or crisis emerges. The third element, the organizational drivers, is interesting to review because when an event or crisis threatens the effects on organizational drivers materializes in different ways. People, for example, can suffer in the near or short term. Processes and materials too, may be affected in different ways over time and all "drivers" that engage at the beginning of a threat response or containment effort must be able to sustain the pressures and requirements needed and last to the end of the effort. Finally, the last feature "performance" merits attention through an event or crisis response effort. Troublesome events and crises challenge a staffs' existing competencies and, in many instances, require them to develop new competencies, skills and talents. Those who meet this need not only provide capable services to the organization through the event management and crisis containment efforts but they clearly may

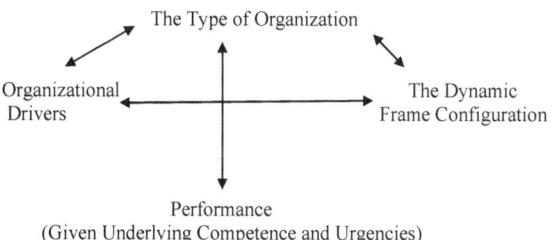

Diagram 2.1 Organizational systemic framework

be better prepared for the post-event or crisis periods and that may be of real long-term benefit to the organization.

As the information in Diagram 2.1 suggests, there is an inter-relationship among these four elements that cannot be dismissed. This implies that if one began to look at an organization from any one of the four elements, the significance of the element would be only meaningful in the ways the other three successfully link with it. The nature and foundation for these points are covered in the material that follows. Beginning with a review of our classification system for organizations, it is possible to see how unique and complex organizations are and why efforts to ensure that the elements of organization function in ways that are truly integrated is important.

Next, the constituent make-up of organizations is examined through a review of what we call "organizational drivers." This is a discussion of the ways actions and activities exist and are demonstrated throughout an organization. In this review we see how it is necessary to examine the collective nature of the "hard" and "soft" features of organizational activities. People, procedures and organizational culture are some of an organization's soft features, but their full meaning is missed if they are discussed without consideration of some of the organization's "hard" features: the material, equipment, products and services around and through which activities occur.

Examination of the organization's "dynamic frame consideration" explores features that both facilitate an organization's operation and existence and, at the same time, makes it susceptible to threats, risks and vulnerabilities that can accompany traumatic events or a crisis. Often when a traumatic event or crisis dominates an organization there is a tendency to develop a singular, myopic focus on what is in front of one's self. This puts the observer at the risk of losing sight of the wider, bigger picture—for example, systemic effects of the event or crisis. It is a classic failure often compared to not seeing the forest from the trees. This segment of the chapter is important in its own right, but its real value may come when, in later chapters, we actually begin to examine organizations in the throes of a crisis.

Finally, we end the chapter with a review of a fourth key organizational feature, performance. Most readers are familiar with material on this topic, but our approach is noteworthy for two reasons. First, we discuss the features and benefits of good or acceptable performance and the features and costs of poor or unacceptable performance. Performance by any individual, department or organization varies from day-to-day. This discussion provides ways to construct useful baseline material when examining organizations in general and certainly for material covered in the book when looking at organizations and their performance in the face of threatening events or crises.

The second aspect of this discussion is one seldom covered and certainly not often, if at all, discussed in texts that examine organizations experiencing a traumatic event or crisis that must be managed or contained in a timely and effective manner. That second aspect is our concept of "change performance." An organization facing a traumatic event or crisis cannot succeed if it approaches the tasks and activities associated with these phenomena with a "performance-as-usual" orientation. In some cases, this means that familiar performance expectations and standards must be abandoned and in other instances, newer performance behaviors and standards implemented. When and how to develop and shift between these two performance standards are the true challenge for both the organization's leadership and those actually doing the work that needs to be done.

Organizations as a Composite of Organizations: The Typology of Organizations

Organizations are classifiable in terms of four generic themes: The Community, the Enterprise, the Team/Groups or, or the Individual Contributor organization.[1] This classification system allows us to recognize the unique nature of organizations while realizing that most organizations share the same same planning, evaluations and management tools and methodologies for design and operations. Using this approach, comparisons across organizations is possible whether they are schools, retail operations, religions, law enforcement or parts of the healthcare industries.

The biggest differences among the four organizational types is the organization's purpose as defined by its mission, assignment or rationale for existence. Community Organizations, for example, strive to achieve a mission. Pursuit of a mission makes this organization distinct because the mission becomes as much a recruiting device as an organizing theme. Membership in these organizations can define jobs or work in terms of the mission and shared common values. These features unify the community organization's membership around a common undertaking; they make it easy to "know what's important" and why. This orientation breeds and nurtures both a particular type of organization and stakeholder base. Religions, the military, police, and schools are in the category as well as communal organizations like sororities, political parties, charities, cults or even politically extremist movements. Like all organizations they need money to operate but that's not their primary reason for existing.

Achieving the organization's mission is a key balance point, for failure to achieve that mission or anything that corrupts the organization's values, principles or ethics associated with the mission puts the community organization's brand at risk. Healthcare organizations that operate as for-profit enterprises have a familiar community organization within their social network, the "charity shop" often run by volunteers. These community organizations within a larger organization often exist to meet or support a particular goal of the larger organization. These organizations may have a mission that seeks to purchase particular equipment or supplies or to contribute to a special organizational fund. Finally, while these organizations are part of the larger organization they also operate as their own separate entity.

In contrast to the community organization, the Enterprise Organization's mission strives to earn money, ideally through profits from its activities; its products and services. Indeed, that same healthcare organization that has a community of volunteers operating to support special functions or services, is itself a very different organization. The two organizations exist in harmony and under the same structure but they are very different entities.

True, many enterprises like to speak about their mission as a business, but everything about their mission is to pursue financial well-being. Values and ideals may be part of the organization's culture but they are not the reasons why the organization exists. And, too, some people belong to an enterprise because they believe in the organization's mission and share the same values but the bottom line for most is that the enterprise is a place to learn new skills, an opportunity for advancement or, simply, it is a job—an income.

One thing all who are employed by an enterprise organization share, however, is that failure to perform as expected, to produce a good product or service, to miss a deadline or important benchmark, can increase risk or vulnerabilities for the organization. For profit hospitals, nursing homes, dentists and related healthcare delivery organizations know this; they see the risks and rewards associated with performance every day. Enterprises exist in a competitive environment with other enterprises as their competitors. Failure to perform as expected has consequences.

A third type of organization is the Team. These organizations also form around a particular mission but there is a finite nature to this organization's activities. The team pursues a mission defined in terms of a specific event, game, client, project or time period. Moreover, the team of individuals that meets for one mission might not be the same team that meets for another mission or game or project or operation. The surgical team that forms for a particular operation may never reconfigure again and even a sport team's starting lineup can vary from game to game and certainly from season to season. Once the game is over, so concludes the team's mission to "win the game."

The make-up of a team is defined by particular skills or competencies. A pitcher on a baseball team may not be a good fielder or batter, a surgeon not a good nurse, nor a sales professional a good technician. Teams form their membership around a particular mission or problem or at a particular time for a specific purpose, and once needs are met the team may disband and not reconfigure in the same way again. It is the nature of this type of organization. However, lose the game and that mission is lost, or if the surgeon loses a patient during the operation then that mission is lost. Sometimes, lose enough games or patients and the damage collects around the organization's brand or individual's reputation. Again, performance is a driver in the team/group organization as well the other organizational types.

Some in organizations mistake operational departments for teams. They will refer to the finance or admissions department as a team, but these are not teams. These departments might be classified as working toward a common objective, but membership in these departments is not grounded in the department's value system, leadership, vision or mission. It is a job, a task or an assignment that defines membership in a department. For example, a nursing home's physical therapy department is built around a specific objective to handle those residents who need some type of physical rehabilitation. Likewise, clinical nursing areas function to meet the special needs of those patients with advanced care issues. Members of the physical therapy or clinical nursing departments may want the department to work as a team (e.g., more communication, collaboration, perhaps a better focus on its mission), but it is not a team as we define it. In each case, their department's function to meet the sometimes on-going needs of a diverse population; it is not pursuit of a mission, per se, it is pursuit of a clinical or business objective.

The final organization type we consider is the Individual Contributor. Nurses, lawyers, doctors, admission clerks, plumbers or car mechanics are examples. They are unique because they can be stand-alone individuals with their own organization or members of a larger organization be it a community, enterprise or team. The CEO and admissions clerk working at a for-profit hospital are individual contributors in an enterprise, the patrol officer on the police force is one, as are the quarterback and tackles on a football team. They are part of a larger organization and they have their own brand or image to develop and maintain or, in the case of a traumatic event or crisis, to protect from becoming distressed.

Finally, these four organizational classifications are useful for a variety of reasons, but three stand out. First, this classification system helps us look at organizations that exist for some particular reason. Sometimes it is to earn a profit for investors other times, as in the case of the community organization, to meet the social, cognitive or emotional needs of its members. Team members use their skills and talents to achieve a mission, to see a project to its successful end; then move on to some other project, game or assignment. Individual contributors can do what they do best across a variety of different types of organizations. They can stand out as individuals and as part of a larger organization.

A second reason these classifications are useful as tools for adding to our understanding of organizations is that, in fact, almost all organizations are a composite, in one way or another, of all four of these entities. We have already seen how a hospital might function as a *for-profit enterprise* while comprised of finance and admission's departments, a volunteer working in *a community or charitable activity*, and a *surgery team* that may specialize in performing a particular type of medical procedure or *doctors, nurses or janitors working as individual contributors* in some support capacity. This is important to understand because it illustrates that all organizations are a combination of different types of distinct sub-organizations, that all of these are definable in terms of there own particular mission and that they must function well if the organization, as a whole, is to manage its risks, threats and vulnerabilities. Under performance in any way and by any one can affect the organization as a whole particularly when faced with threats associated with a troublesome event or crisis.

This classification system provides a means for understanding the underlying order defining an organization and its operations. Once classified, it is possible to get a sense for the various departments needed for the organization to function, and this then points to the duties or tasks for those in each department. Combined, this helps anticipate the products and services associated with performance and the levels of performance needed for the organization's success. It provides a sense for the nature of and relationships among internal and external stakeholders which comprise the full make-up of organizational performance and, lastly, use of these classifications provides insight into the ways effects of an event or crisis can travel through the organization's social network. This last point is of particular interest because a troublesome event or crisis can emerge anywhere within an organization, which is another reason why information and communication systems are of critical importance to an organization. A seemingly insignificant event in the billing department related to a contested bill can send ripples through an organization in ways that are hard to predict. Yet, if the event triggers a crisis, the results can be significant.

Internal Organizational Drivers

Unrecognized risks and vulnerabilities associated with day-to-day operations are distressing and dangerous phenomena in the healthcare industry. Our approach to crises begins with understanding their source, why they emerge in the first place. This orientation places mismanaged events at the center of our preliminary forensic examinations. With this claim made, the central notion for those in leadership positions to recognize is that the array of potential triggering events in any organization is staggering.

Rude personnel, negligent service delivery, potentially dangerous environments or a lack of pre-emptive thinking regarding the organization and its stakeholders are sources for troublesome events. Give yourself a minute and look at any hospital, nursing home or other healthcare facility with which you are familiar and ask yourself what you would identify as a "troublesome" part of its operations. Walk in through its parking lot, then into the facility and look for potential risks, threats and vulnerabilities; things you might change if you were in charge. When doing this, consider things that if managed differently might turn the organization in a different, perhaps safer direction. We ask this question now because one of the most prominent features of an organization is its "*organizational drivers*"; the people, processes, material and equipment, management or the organization's culture, that define the organization as a functional entity.

An organization's network, per se, is an arbitrary tool for describing links and relationships among the organization's diverse population. Table 2.1 illustrates what the make-up of a typical network might look like for a healthcare organization. In the table note that the list of drivers is expanded to reflect the dynamic nature of these organizations. Finance is a driver for all for-profit organizations and certainly a component or need for all organizations. The role of "rules and regulations," however, can differ widely across organizations. Healthcare organizations, for example, are rule-governed versus rule-guided organizations. This means that healthcare organizations must perform and are often licensed under various local, state and federal rules. Violation of rules and regulations can result in penalties or different disciplinary actions.

Table 2.1 A representative summary of performance drivers

	Healthcare organizations
People—Patients	Individuals requiring routine or acute medical assistance
People—Administration	Hospital Administrator /CEO
	Chief of Staff
	Chief Operating Officer
	Chief Financial Officer/Controller
	Chief Information Officer Chief Nursing Executive/Nursing Staff
	Department Directors for: Human Resources, Admissions, Labs, Social Services, Pharmaceutical Services, Dietary Services, Maintenance & Housekeeping Director
People—Staffing	Medical & Nursing Staff
	Business Office, Purchasing
	Information Management Staff including Medical Records
	Human Resources, Training & Development
	Admissions, Social Services, Dietary Services, Pharmaceutical Services
	Laboratory/Radiology, Physical Therapy
	Maintenance & Housekeeping
People—Leadership	Executive Level Officers, Corporate Boards of Directors and Trustees
	Advisors and Consultants
Processes: How they work	Individuals are cared for on an acute basis, the length of time depending on the care needs. The typical length of stay in the US is 4.5 days. Upon admission, individuals are assessed for severity and triaged to different departments where further specialized care is given. Upon discharge, patients may return home or transferred to a sub-acute rehab facility.

(continued)

Table 2.1 (continued)

	Healthcare organizations
Material needs	Forms, documentation, databases
Equipment & Facility needs	Hospital beds, ventilators, defibrillators, surgical and exam tables, furniture, laboratory diagnostic and imaging equipment, specialized equipment (e.g. spirometer), surgical equipment, sterilizers, lighting, laundry, computers, treatment rooms, wheelchairs/walkers, health monitors (e.g., blood pressure), fire and safety equipment, protective equipment
	Equipment to supply each of the following areas: Imaging, laboratory, surgery, ICU, outpatient department, pharmacy, each specialized department (e.g. ENT, Cardiac), ER/ED, Maternity, PT/OT/Speech therapy, mortuary equipment, maintenance, kitchen, laundry
Financing	Depends largely on how their patients are insured e.g. privately (e.g. through employers), Medicare (covering seniors and some of those with disabilities), Medicaid (for low income individuals), and charitable donations. Public hospitals are also funded through tax payer dollars
Rules & Regulations	Governed by state and federal regulations to be a licensed facility with hundreds of regulatory requirements
Organizational Culture	Directed from a parent organization
	May be particular within departments or May reflect "outside" elements
	Influenced by other organizations: Government agencies, unions, etc.

Lastly, note that all organizational performance is guided by the make-up of its social network. Stakeholders in these networks are, in many ways, the object of the organization's performance. Failure to perform in ways that meet stakeholder needs can result in an array of problems, not the least of which are troublesome events or crises.

Close examination of the types of personnel and clients served by this organization begins to reveal the inherent complexities associated with operations at any given time and within any given area. Personnel in organizations match both the nature of the work needed to meet customer needs and, of course, the types of clients served. Striking differences among organizations become apparent when looking at factors that define how those in the organization deliver their services, and the tools and resources needed in those efforts. These distinctions are important anytime and particularly when the organizations are managing a troublesome event or attempting to contain a crisis.

Once again, stakeholder-dependent needs define every aspect of organizations and their operations. Performance tailored to meet a stakeholder's needs defines patterns in the organization's operations: from operating as financial business center to the delivery of goods and services. The patterns are similar for all types of organizations but what is different for skilled healthcare centers is that in these organizations, their clients can have physical, emotional or psychological needs and limitations associated with any physical needs. This layering of health conditions dramatically affects how the organization responds to them if a traumatic event or crisis occurs. If a fire, for example, occurs in an office building those in the building can simply be instructed to evaluate the building. That is not always an option in a healthcare organization when clients may be incapacitated, unable to walk without assistance or special equipment or, are slow to move because of their age or health conditions.

Dynamic Organizational Framework

The previous section focused on typical, specific elements associated with "getting the job done." The people, processes, material and equipment, leadership and organizational culture that supports those who are part of the organization's internal or external social networks were the focus. This section examines the broader factors that also affect an organization's performance, its organizational framework.

Diagram 2.2 illustrates one approach to describing an organization's systemic framework. It illustrates a network of existing and potential relationships among different stakeholders. This type of tool is useful when wanting to examine an organization's operations during routine periods and/or when speculating about ways the impact of a troublesome event or, worse, a crisis may affect the organization's social network. For example, examining an organization's systemic framework can indicate who is a typical member of the organization's social network and who enters because of a particular event or crisis?

In the stakeholder social network, we see the players but not their broader demographic make-up or the context in which they operate. To understand these important features we need to examine three other organizational framework devices: the organization's architecture, its operational practices and the organization's brand. These merit special attention because each is critical to an organization's overall performance processes, capacity to deliver products and services and, as a means for bonding relationships between the organization as an entity and its

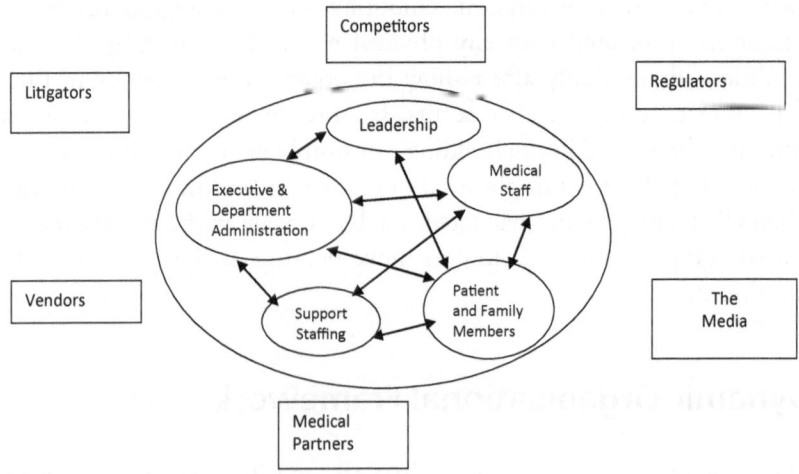

Diagram 2.2 A healthcare organization's internal stakeholders (with some external stakeholders noted)

various stakeholders. Finally, because of their importance to the organization as a whole and their exposure during stressful times, damage to these areas may be a significant byproduct of a traumatic event or crisis.

The first of these devices is the organization's architecture. For example, Trevor and Varcoe,[2] summarized an organization's purpose ("what we do and why we do it"), its business strategy, organizational capability, resource architecture ("what makes us good") and management systems as features associated with the overall architecture. These, for Trevor and Varcoe, comprise the organization's value chain and as such connect with organizational elements throughout the firm. Clearly this value chain is a positive feature but it also points to a vulnerability for the organization should one or more of these chain elements be damaged by a crisis.

Other researchers, for example, writers associated with learn.org[3] see organizational architecture as referring "to the structure and form by which a business operates. All types of businesses, from marketing firms to corporate restaurant chains, operate under this concept." For these authors "organizational architecture is similar to brick-and-mortar architecture, although it deals with concepts instead of building materials. Organizational architecture ensures that all components of a business function cohesively to achieve its goals."

Our preference is to be specific about information and communication channels, hierarchy, value chains or other tangible organizational features as part of its architecture but regardless of your orientation, the primary takeaway is that preference for one of these descriptions over the others is a matter of choice, given the nature of the business. From our point of view all have merit, particularly when considering an organization exposed to a threatening event or emerging crisis. Then, the important thing is to understand how the organizational architecture is affected and what this means to the organization's current and future performance. Those leading an organization should know the status of its architecture before, during and after experiencing a threatening event or crisis.

A second set of framework factors central to an organization's operations are its critical operational practices. These factors serve as both

Table 2.2 A sense of urgency and critical operational practices

Critical operational practices & description	The practice's impact on an individual's sense of urgency in routine settings	The practice's impact on sense of urgency given an organization's challenges, risks & threats
Communication Practices & Strategy are used to, exchange information between or among individuals, groups, and organizations	Communicate goals, issues, and processes. Used to build relationships, to confront issues. Communication reduces avoidance strategies and conflict	Communication is expected. Communication practices show up in programs (e.g., mediation and bargaining), processes and procedures
Evaluations Practices & Strategies are used for research and systematic evaluation of performance, projects or processes. Evaluation practices help planning, decision-making, and problem-solving	Focus is on performance not personalities. Individuals know how efforts, strategies, relationships are assessed. Evaluations look back and ahead. Evaluation criteria make goals meaningful, encourage communication	Evaluation practices underscore risk taking and goal achievement. Goals are achieved against defined performance criteria and through prudent risk taking. "Tempered urgency"
Knowledge Practices & Strategies are used to acquire, build develop, maintain knowledge, skills and competencies	When one has needed skills and competencies one can act. Practices help problem-solving, decision-making. Knowledge enables moves beyond thinking to action	Knowledge practices add depth to the organization. A key practice for the Triple-E: Enabling, enriching, empowering
Relationship Practices & Strategies are used to acquire, build, develop, and maintain relationships	Relationships and networks are critical for urgency. Relationships expand competency capabilities	Good relationships promote urgency. Some programs include customers; urgency expands the organization's reach
Performance Practices & Strategies are used to introduce, propel and/or guide operations and ensure that performance meets goals, objectives, and standards	Urgency is part of all personal and group/team planning, goal setting, design, & mission activities. Urgency found in priorities, strategy, tactics, & tasks. People know what's expected and when	Urgency requires attention to detail, plans for evaluation and follow-up activities. Consistency and reliability increase with solid performance practices

Critical operational practices & description	The practice's impact on an individual's sense of urgency in routine settings	The practice's impact on sense of urgency given an organization's challenges, risks & threats
Information, Evaluation & Confirmation Practices & Strategies support infrastructure and information management practices facilitate all strategic practices. Both formal and informal	Information is critical for urgency. It's used to define issues, to seek out solutions and problem-solving channels; for confirming and evaluating progress and results	Priorities, needs, conditions are communicated via information channels and networks. Practices facilitate progress assessments. Availability, accuracy, and accessibility of information are critical for urgency

a bond and link for the stakeholders inside and outside the organization. Table 2.2 summarizes six of these practices in three ways.[4] The first column offers a standard definition of each practice. These definitions illustrate the role of the practices and the potential contribution of each to stakeholders. It is important to note that no one practice is more important that another, although some may play a greater role depending on the organization. An organization's leadership should be able to demonstrate ways the practices are in place across all departments.

The next two columns provide important information for all in an organization and particularly those in leadership positions and/or involved in the management of a threatening event or emerging crisis. The table's information is valuable because it outlines ways practices are reflected in daily work or activities and/or, when those in an organization are expected to respond to a threatening event or emerging crisis. This is a very important point: An individual's behavior must reflect a sense of urgency combined with the behavior, decisions, and action appropriate to the situation at hand. These practices, in other words, are gateways for individuals to successfully apply their skills and experience to any situation, whether the need is routine or unique.

The practices are used proactively and sometimes in a pre-emptive manner. Consider, for example, the use of communication practices. Communications should be accurate, complete and timely when part of daily interactions but in a crisis, augment communications to include perspective, the scope and scale of a situation and conclusions or recommendations. An individual's behaviors in routine and extreme situations are performance indicators that reveal the individual's competencies, unique characteristics like judgment, personal values, commitment and affiliation and, of course, the demands created because of the event or crisis.

Demonstration of behavior around these key practices is telling. For example, think of the conclusions one might draw about an individual in an administrative position who skips over evaluation or assessment practices or who does not value knowledge or relationship practices? Or, how might an orientation to these and other key practices surface in quality, safety or security programs designed to enhance healthcare delivery? Finally, in what ways might an individual's orientation to these practices contribute to the organization's or its stakeholders' potential risk, threat and vulnerability thresholds? These practices are not "nice to have" organizational features; they are "musts" for people and organizations. Failure to approach an organization's operations without this level of certainty or commitment may result in a damaged or traumatized architecture or operational environment.

Measuring Operational Practices

Measurement, evaluation and assessments are a regular feature of proactive organizations and they are a primary interest when dealing with events or crises. This noted, it makes sense to look back over the material presented to assess the fit, contribution and meaningfulness of assessments for healthcare organizations generally and for particular departments in particular. Conducting assessment audits can vary in scope and scale but, overall, the process is straightforward. For example, here is one way to develop a flexible, easy to administer assessment process.

Begin by applying a scale (for example, ranging from 1 = low to 5 = high) to use for each practice. Next, pick out two or three examples of the use of the operational practices in a particular department or the overall organization. For example, safety, security or quality programs might be a good focal point when evaluating performance practices in risky areas. In this instance, it may be sufficient to simply examine the extent to which safety practices are followed or that quality standards are in place and followed, then each is rated given the scale used. For example, are safety audits conducted within the target area? Are the audits fair or biased?

Examining and analyzing audits of all of the practices categories in Table 2.2 may provide insightful information regarding the organization or a particular department. For example, one important criterion to look at when assessing anything in an organization, and certainly operational practices, is the alignment with the organization's vision and mission. To what extent does an evaluation score reflect ways adhering to a particular practice contributes to the organization achieving its vision or mission? This level of information is valuable whether the organization is using the information as part of a general assessment or for specific pre-emptive means.

Second, in what ways does a practice make a genuine contribution to the organization? Sometimes the contribution is limited, for example at the department or individual level. That is fine. But the issue here is not to target any particular department or individual but rather demonstrate ways the practices provide overall benefits to a department or the organization. Effective meetings contribute to improved communication, information management and problem-solving so, do those who conduct meetings demonstrate a need for coaching in meeting management.

Next, seek to understand ways the practices make different contributions to an area. Operational practice should not be an overwhelming or unnecessary burden but rather something that contributes to the work to be done or the effort extended. Are the practices suitable and reasonable? Do they make sense? For example, security practices may be part of all organizational areas but, at the same time, they can be more important in areas where security is a most important issue. Note the extent to which practices add specific or range of value to the organization. An improved working environment where people communicate and collaborate on problems adds value to the area and the organization as a whole.

Can stakeholders follow and demonstrate the practices in their own organizations? How are the practices demonstrated throughout the organization? Are they manageable, within employee capabilities? Do some practices require special skills or training to follow? Should the oversight of particular practices be handled by contractors or outside firms? Building security is one example and computer security is another. The point here is that if having particular practices in place is important then the training and support needed to develop the desired practices also is important.

An Organization's Brand or Image as a Performance Driver

A dominant feature of elements defining an organization's structural framework is the inter-relationship among elements of the organization's structure. An organization's architecture provides a context for operational practices, and both contribute to the organization's image or brand. This last feature is particularly unique, however, in that an organization's brand exists in two distinct states: One defined by the organization and a second that is the product of the stakeholder's personal perception of the organization.

Consider this point in terms of a hospital or other healthcare delivery organization. Those operating a particular hospital have their own idea or image of the organization. The leaders, administrators or staff members might see their organization as an excellent example of what, for example, quality healthcare should and does look like. They may believe that their programs, practices and staff model this image in their work, and that promotional publications and other material reflect this image. This is one perspective of an organization's brand or image.

Next, regardless of what the organization's stakeholders believe, this does not mean that current or prospective patients will share the same image. This is because an organization's brand or image is a product of an individual's perception; it is a personal construct that individuals create and use to plan, design, control and, explain personal actions or beliefs.[5] This makes an organization's brand a very personal feature for individuals and something that may be very different from the view those associated with the organization see it as being.

An organization's brand is a valuable contributor to the organization's success. If the public or stakeholders believe in the organization's brand, they may support it in a number of different ways, for example by buying or using its products and services. In the case of a healthcare organization, stakeholders that support the organization's brand or image may see the organization as a place for their entire family to receive healthcare as they age or if they become incapacitated.[6]

A strong brand also may help the organization's leadership manage negative press coverage during a traumatic event or crisis. Stakeholders strongly aligned with the organization's brand may transfer that alignment to the organization's leadership and the decisions leaders make. It is a type of "halo effect." Perceptions of the organization's credibility are transferred to those who work for the organization simply because that where they work.

But an organization's brand, like its architecture and operations is susceptible to damage associated with a traumatic event or crisis. Damage here, however, is not easily rectified; unlike physical features of an organization the brand is not a feature that can be easily repaired or replaced. Moreover, and to add complexity to matters related to a damaged brand, because an organization's brand is defined by individuals, trying to come up with one or even a few treatments for the damaged brand may be virtually impossible. Brand "repair" becomes something the individual stakeholders do for themselves, whether they are part of the organization's internal or external social networks.

Tafoya[7] coined the term, "brand trauma" to describe the wide-sweeping damages a brand might experience because of a traumatic event or crisis. The phenomenon is unique for a number of reasons, but one that an organization's leadership may find of most interest are the factors Tafoya isolated that contribute to this phenomenon and subsequent damage to the organization's image. Table 2.3 summarizes seven contributors to brand trauma Tafoya observed and at least five of those may be immediately associated with a threatening event or crisis.[8]

Items 1, 3, 4, 5 and 7 are particularly important because when an event triggers a crisis any stress on architectural and operational features triggers potential damage to the organization's brand. Organizations are rich, dynamic systems and few things demonstrate the organization's susceptibility to damage like a mismanaged event or emerging crisis.

Table 2.3 Seven contributors to Brand Trauma

1. Poor management of negative events
2. Indifference to the brand; Its role in the organization isn't recognized
3. Loss of focus, synergy; Key organizational elements are not aligned
4. Brand drift: failure to manage and update the brand
5. Carelessness, inattention
6. Brand displacement (by another brand, the need no longer exists, etc.)
7. Conflict: internal or external
(Tafoya 2018, p. 86)

Summarizing the Relationship Among Organizational Operations, Architecture and Brand

Table 2.4 summarizes ways in which an organization's operational, architectural and brand features link to each other, the organization's networks and stakeholders. In the table we see that events and crises carry potential risks for these organizational components and the organization itself. It is also important to note that once these are exposed to risk, the potential for damage to the organization can be direct and widespread. Next, and perhaps most problematic, is that once the trauma associated with risk and damage spreads through the internal and external networks, controlling negative effects may be virtually impossible. Finally, when reviewing the information in Tables 2.3 and 2.4 as a means for

Table 2.4 Mapping the relationship between operational, architectural, Brand Trauma, and risk

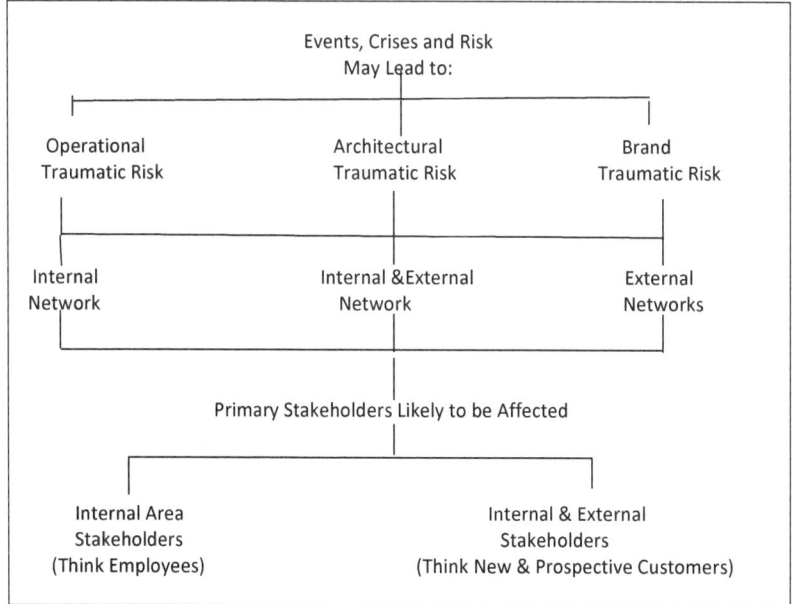

understanding what triggered the trauma, we see that a common link is individual performance, a theme discussed next.

Performance and Its Measurement

Organizations and individuals demonstrate their performance in active and passive ways. Simply acquiring and maintaining equipment, materials, processes and practices that comprise an organization's operations is a passive way for demonstrating the potential for performance. Telephone systems, websites, billing procedures and the like are representative passive performance centers. However, a more proactive way for demonstrating performance is through the use of the organization's physical features in combination with staff to meet stakeholder needs. This is performance associated with people; those working in support of the organization and those who operate as its adversaries. In either case, people, through their behavior and performance can influence organizations.

Regardless of the type of organization, we are concentrating on performance in two instances: Performance associated with daily, routine activities and performance when responding to a traumatic event or emerging crisis. We will conclude this chapter by reviewing facets of performance that should be associated with all organizational and individual activity and especially when anticipating or responding to a traumatic event or emerging crisis. These performance areas are obviously important so the best way to monitor and gauge their effectiveness is by regularly assessing them.

Assessments or evaluations can eliminate questions or guesswork associated with performance. Statements like "we could have done better," "our plans didn't work" or, "we need more resources" are virtually meaningless on their own. What does "better" mean? Who could have done better? What could have been done better? Do we mean that everything should have been done better or just doing better in some areas is what is needed? And which plans "didn't work?" All plans or emergency plans? Preliminary plans or plans designed to address a particular part of the event or crisis? And what about the resources? Do we need more resources or specific resources in certain areas at certain times? Are we talking about people, equipment, material, monetary or temporal resources? Good evaluations replace hunches, guesses and ambiguities with tangible facts and information.

Second, assessments and evaluation aid planning, design, decision-making and implementation strategies and tactics. As you will see in the next chapter, we believe that crises do not happen by accident or as "acts of God." We believe that crises are triggered when people mismanage events. Preventing mismanagement can be enhanced with improved assessments and evaluations. Virtually everything about the human factor in successful "event management" is linked to planning, design, decision-making and implementation. Improve your assessment skills and competencies and you can contribute to improved performance.

Finally, if communication was identified as part of effective operational practices, communication is certainly enhanced with the use of performance assessments and evaluations. Information derived from assessments and evaluations help people work toward agreement, toward consensus. Assessments and evaluations are driven by an interest in satisfying needs, wants and desires for people looking for answers. Information, communication, facts, details, what works, what doesn't, attitudes, opinions and beliefs are just a short list of what people bring to a meeting when faced with a troublesome event or impending crisis. Effective and meaningful assessments and evaluations provide baselines and referent points for discussions. People, particularly in leadership roles, should not avoid or resist evaluations and assessments. Rather they should promote and embrace their evaluations and assessments as core activities for the organization and its stakeholders. The focus is on identifying problems and solutions, not finger pointing.

Conclusion: Performance Management Targets

We end this chapter by returning to material introduced earlier. Table 2.5 outlines areas to consider when doing performance assessments. This is only an illustration but, at the same time, it useful to speculate on how

Table 2.5 Representative (and ideal) performance criteria for evaluations in a healthcare organization

Assessment area	Performance criteria and hypothetical targets
People—Patients	• Receiving prescribed care • Receiving prescribed medication • No avoidable accidents *Target: Performance levels meet/exceed expectations*
People—Professional Staff	• Effective and timely staff meetings • Timely problem or issue management • Maintain building census *Target: Performance levels meet/exceed expectations*
People—Staffing	• Performance of prescribed duties • Training and certification required are complete • Levels of performance at "meets" or "exceeds" levels • Reduced turnover • Exceptional performance during emergencies • Response time to emergency/call response system with residents *Target: Performance levels exceed expectations*
People—Leadership	• Effective and timely staff meetings • Timely problem or issue management • Maintain building census *Target: Performance levels exceed expectations*
Processes: How they work	• Safety programs in place and evaluated • Quality programs in place and evaluated • Security programs in place and evaluated • Customer service programs in place and evaluated • Operational practices in place and evaluated *Target: Performance levels exceed expectations*
Material needs	• Needed materials in place and evaluated • Materials for special needs in place and evaluated *Target: Performance levels exceed expectations*

(continued)

Table 2.5 (continued)

Assessment area	Performance criteria and hypothetical targets
Equipment & Facility needs	• Necessary medical equipment on hand
	• Necessary equipment/supplies for repairs and renovations
	Target: Performance levels exceed expectations
Financing	• Track private pays vs insurance pays
	• Maintain funds for planned and unforeseen expenditures
	Target: Performance levels exceed expectations
Rules & Regulations	• Defined and followed
	• Part of new hire training and orientation
	• Part of all special program
	Target: Performance levels meet/exceed expectations
Organizational Culture	• Encourage feedback from all employees
	• Employee satisfaction
	Target: Performance levels meet/exceed expectations

each individual line item might be valued and how different individuals might value them given their positions or their own values. This last point is especially interesting. If, say all the members of a department completed assessments based on this type of table what might the results look like? Where is there consensus and where are there disagreements? Do particular assessment areas receive better ratings than others and, if so, why? Finally, what does information associated with these assessments reveal about the organization's strengths, weaknesses and vulnerabilities?

The post-assessment discussion might be an interesting way to uncover existing misperceptions, where training might be useful or, how responses might vary when thinking of these performance criteria for routine matters versus those times when dealing with a troublesome event or crisis. Notice that the evaluations do not focus solely on people but include processes and practices as well. Also note that where and when people are included in the assessments that the organization's leadership is included along with professional and support staffs. Finally, since this is an organizational assessment also included are aspects of the organization's culture, processes, procedures and practices.

Finally, this particular example is of a "high-level" assessment. If it seems necessary to get specific insight into operations, the same type of assessment can be prepared for department or division level assessments. This level of analysis not only provides a glimpse into a particular department's operations but, if all or most departments are assessed at the same time, it is possible to make comparisons across all departments on all key assessment areas. Again, the issue is not "finger pointing," the issue is identifying problems or issues needing to be addressed. The particular value in these types of assessments will be clear once you begin to study material in the next chapter.

Notes

1. Tafoya, Dennis W. *The Effective Organization: Practical Application of Complexity Theory and Organizational Design to Maximize Performance in the Face of Emerging Events.* NY: Routledge, 2010.
2. Trevor, Jonathan and Barry Varcoe. "How Aligned Is Your Organization?" *Harvard Business Review*, February 2017, https://hbr.org/2017/02/how-aligned-is-your-organization.
3. Trevor, Jonathan and Barry Varcoe. "What Is Organizational Architecture." Learn.org, accessed October 30, 2020, https://learn.org/articles/What_is_Organizational_Architecture.
4. Tafoya, Dennis. *The Effective Organization.* New York: Routledge, 2010.
5. Kelly, G. A. *The Psychology of Personal Constructs.* New York: Norton, 1955.
6. Tafoya, Dennis. *Organizations in the Face of Crisis: Managing the Brand and Stakeholders.* New York: Palgrave/Macmillan, 2013 and Tafoya, Dennis W. *Crisis, Catastrophe, and Disaster in Organizations: Managing Threats to Operations, Architecture, Brand and Stakeholders.* New York: Palgrave/Macmillan, 2020.
7. Tafoya, Dennis W. *Managing Organizational Crisis and Brand Trauma.* New York: Palgrave/Macmillan, 2018.
8. Ibid., p. 86.

3

From Events to Crises, Catastrophes and Disaster: Before the Collapse

Abstract When first looking at an event or crisis, our initial inclination is to speculate and construct conclusions regarding what occurred and why. These conclusions are often premature. We may believe we see the nature of the occurrence; its scope, scale and basic elements. However, behind the observable event or crisis are other details we can only begin to describe. And, as if to truly challenge the complexities associated with our observations and conclusions, there are other details we do not see at all and about which we may not even be able to speculate. Our interest in this chapter is to examine ways to build a plan that helps those involved in event management or crisis containment activities better understand their tasks and make the best decisions possible.

Keywords The event spectrum · The crisis · Catastrophe and disaster model · Phenom stream · Stakeholder network · Organizational capabilities and competencies · Event management · Crisis containment

Introduction: When first looking at an event or crisis, our initial inclination is to speculate and construct conclusions regarding what occurred and why. These conclusions are often premature. We may believe we see the nature of the occurrence; its scope, scale and basic elements. However, behind the observable event or crisis are other details we can only begin to describe. And, as if to truly challenge the complexities associated with our observations and conclusions, there are other details we do not see at all and about which we may not even be able to speculate.

Decision-making is an everyday occurrence in organizations. Our interest in this chapter is to examine ways to build a plan that helps those involved in event management or crisis containment activities better understand their tasks and make the best decisions possible. Our model is straightforward and defined by four objectives. First, understanding the background for an event and/or crisis is critical. This includes both knowing their nature and what could have led to successful management and containment efforts. Next, isolate the demand design decisions. What led to the designed approach and, of course, with what results? Third, evaluate the decisions and decision process that led to action taken or, not taken. Finally, what happened once the action plan was launched or if not launched what action was taken.

The Event Spectrum and the Crisis, Catastrophe and Disaster Model

There is a clear relationship between events and crises. To begin with, our models suggest that the mismanagement of an event triggers a crisis. Consider any of the following occurring for a hospital or healthcare organization: There is fire in a building, a bus carrying residents of a nursing home on a day trip crashes or a hurricane sweeps through the community causing an array of damages. These are not crises; they are events. The management of each defines if a crisis is triggered.

Difficulties for the problem solver are further complicated because the event may have several underlying issues associated with it. Consider the information in Table 3.1 and the three events noted above. Once a discovery process launches associated with a fire a number of factors

Table 3.1 Representative activities when responding to an event

The nature of the event is identified
A discovery process begins to understand what happened and why
Possible actions to take are outlined
A selected action(s) is taken
There are results associated with the action(s) taken
There are consequences

may be surface related to the event. Perhaps locked fire doors prevented escape so lives were lost and injuries escalated. The bus crash may be related to the bus' brakes; they may not have been serviced. Perhaps the driver has a bad driving record with a history of traffic violations. Was the driver using a cell phone? Did a passenger distract the driver?

Hurricanes are dramatic events. Flooding, damage to buildings or just the loss of power can be debilitating events for a healthcare facility. Why do these events associated with the storm have their effects? How long did it take to evacuate buildings? Were buildings in a flood zone? Were staff trained to manage this type of event? The hurricane is the event, not the crisis. The crisis is the phenomenon that emerges because of actions associated with the event.

Next, even if actions were taken, were they the best to take given the event, the people and facilities involved? In all three of the sample events discussed, people were exposed to potential harm. For example, fire forces residents of a nursing home or hospital to leave their rooms or buildings and to go out in what may be a cold, rainy night. Now the original event is layers with other factors which may increase the potential for harm and, in turn, the triggering of a crisis for some or all effected.

Secondary events add to an event's significance as a phenomenon to manage. These secondary or sub-events, also need management. Injuries in the fire, the bus accident or hurricane events may turn into life-threatening crises if not addressed in a timely manner. But the reason time is a factor in these instances is that the passage of time allows for the secondary events to surface as issues also needing to be managed to avoid a cascade of crises from emerging. People evacuate a building because of a fire and face illness because of exposure to the cold or because time passes before they receive treatment for smoke inhalation. If the bus accident leaves people bleeding along the roadside, threats to their lives increase as time passes without aid. Failure to evacuate a building prior to the hurricane's arrival may lead to flooding and loss of power, which strands those in the building from aid and increases their exposure to the storm. If you begin to model the risk associated with each of these events you will start to see risk exposures increase with the passage of time and the emergence of unaddressed sub-events. It is important to note that the decision not to act or to delay action in the face of a troublesome event may be as significant as a poor decision in the face of the same event.

Each of the three events discussed can trigger a crisis for the stakeholders involved if not managed effectively and then, of course, any resulting crisis can spawn additional events. In short, every event has the potential to trigger a potentially dangerous stream of occurrences, incidents or episodes. If the hurricane damages the building, its phone or computer networks, these must be repaired before operations can return to normal. If the same storm damaged patient records, then another level of negative effects arises. Now, in addition to damage to the building, operations are crippled or forced to stop until repairs are complete. And, of course, there is the organization's image or brand. What will local residents think about the organization's approach to safety or the management capabilities of its staff? In addition, if reports of potential litigation appear in the media, possible doubt regarding the organization and its management can spread. Ultimately, why should anyone believe that the care, custody and control of their loved ones to those who operate these facilities? A conclusion: Just because someone took action in the face of an event that does not mean that actions taken reflect good decisions.

Those faced with the task of managing an event quickly see some of the potential circumstances they may face: events differ in complexity and, as a result, require different skills and competencies for their management. Consider the "event spectrum" described in Table 3.2.[1] Most events needing attention in organizations are routine, part of the job. Systems and programs often can be implemented to anticipate these events should they materialize. This is one reason why organizations have training programs, performance management systems and performance reviews. These are tools to help staff prepare for the effective and efficient management of routine matters.

Table 3.2 The spectrum of events: Poor event management is a primary catalyst for the emergence of a crisis

Event Type One: Routine, anticipated, even planned for events which unfold within the framework of general activity. **Example**: Sales or recruiting events, assembly activities, personnel reviews, sales transactions, rituals
Event Type Two: Unanticipated events which emerge but are within the framework of organizational or general activity. **Example**: Customer complaints, employee theft, celebrations, disciplinary actions, loss of key personnel
Event Type Three: Extraordinary events that are within the organization's horizon but may be anticipated, planned for. **Example**: Loss of key person, fire in a manufacturing facility, layoffs, on-site injury
Event Type Four: Extraordinary events that are within the organization's horizon but typically not be anticipated or planned for. **Example**: New technology, loss of key stakeholders, discrimination claims, aggressive driving, defections, sabotage
Event Type Five: Extraordinary events beyond the scope of an organization that may be anticipated or planned for. **Example**: Terrorist attacks or "regional" natural disasters.
Event Type Six: Extraordinary events beyond the scope of organization that are not typically planned for or anticipated. **Example**: Unethical behavior by externals (e.g., lawyers, doctors), shooting of one employee by another employee

(Tafoya, 2010, p. 138)

Next, consider Event "Type Two." Despite all of the planning, training and discussions in organizations, unanticipated things happen. It is hard to predict when a customer or client might complain about service received but it happens. And what about an employee theft? Even with the best background checks, peoples' lives and needs change so an employee may see theft as a possible solution to their situation. Unanticipated events must be managed, but sometimes those in the organization have little experience dealing with them. Options exist, of course, and that is why organizations learn to rely on and use consultants, lawyers, outside accountants and other professionals; this is a way to extend the organization's competencies in order to manage unanticipated events.

The third type of event is extraordinary but they also are events that may be planned for, even if there is no reason to expect they will occur. Areas within the organization's Human Resource departments devote time and energy building programs to meet current and unforeseen

staffing needs. If there is an unexpected staff shortage, these departments can move quickly to address the emerging need. Hiring is another
example of a managed event. If done well, for example without bias for
race or sex, then the hiring becomes a routine event and may avoid a
crisis.

"Event Type Four covers extraordinary events that are within the organization's horizon, but typically not be anticipated or planned for by the
organization's staff. These types of events can carry higher levels of risk
for the organization, and with higher risks, any emerging crisis associated with poor management can result in debilitating exposures. Here,
again, use of outside resources with technical or professional expertise
(e.g., lawyers and consultants) can help manage these events; it becomes
a far-sighted, pre-emptive approach.

However, these types of events reveal another potential weakness in
organizations, the failure to maintain professional competencies. Trade
journals, professional associations or accreditation requirements are valuable ways to help staff stay abreast of changes in their industry or
professions. It is not prudent to believe that the education or degree
earned even five years ago is sufficient to help one manage changes in
a dynamic working environment. Yet, some in organizations do not see
the value in letting their staff attend conferences ("penny wise..."), or
only let those staff required to have annual certification for their work
attend outside programs. What is interesting about event type four is that
when many in organizations complain of an event "blindsiding them" in
fact, it may have been their own personal or organizational cultures that
facilitated the surfacing of these risk exposures.

Event types Five and Six are obviously significant occurrences. Indeed,
many inside and outside the organization might feel sorry for those who
experience exposure to these types of events. They are significant events
yet, at the same time, they must be managed and managed effectively in
order to stave off a crisis.

Moreover, despite the fact that these are truly extraordinary events
they also are familiar to most professionals. Our research has indicated
that these types of events occur in organizations less than five percent of
the time when compared to other events. This could give an organization's leadership a false sense of security. However, these are potentially

events of considerable magnitude and complexity so should they occur the effects may be drastic. These events demand media coverage. They are the types of events that can hang in the news or social media channels for weeks, and if caught up in litigation or tragedies like loss of life, for months and years. So, at least from an "events management and crisis avoidance perspective" it makes sense to both know about, to think about and wonder how well prepared your organization might be in order to manage this level of threat.

Understanding why mismanagement of an event occurred and triggered a crisis begins with understanding the nature of both the event and/or crisis. What information regarding the nature of the event is available, what are typical characteristics of the event that needs management, what research is needed to build a plan of action? To illustrate these points consider the events in Table 3.3.

The events in Table 3.3 are examples of routine events one might encounter in any healthcare facility. A wet floor, a very clean, waxed floor, an individual in a hurry to get to a meeting may contribute to a fall. It is a routine event so what action(s) might help manage the event? The point behind the examples in Table 3.3 is that any event presents an

Table 3.3 When routine events become notable events

Representative events	Investigation needed to establish the cause (Add your own thoughs)	Possible actions to take
A Visitor falls		Do nothing
		Have someone else do something
		Do something yourself
Fire in the building		Do nothing
		Have someone else do something
		Do something yourself
Patient dies		Do nothing
		Have someone else do something
		Do something yourself
Patient develops pneumonia		Do nothing
		Have someone else do something
		Do something yourself

observer with choices regarding the actions to take, even if the action is avoidance, to do nothing.

Even apart from the direct action one might take in response to an event, all events present members of the organization with other ancillary actions to take in response to the situation. Routine or seemingly insignificant events necessitate the collection of basic information in order to keep the organization's leadership informed. This information informs the organization's leadership about what happened but the same information is useful when building a pool of material associated with the organization's risk profile. For example, are staff members trained to handle these and other routine events? Have administrators and staff ever made an attempt to list the types of routine events that might occur given their residents, their facilities or the nature of their business? In addition, how does the organization's leadership know that the training, programs and processes in place to address routine events, or any events for that matter, will have their desired effects? And, finally, if the organization's leadership thought about their own responses to the incidents in Table 3.3 how would their responses compare with those of the organization's staff? Where are the differences and does it matter if there are differences? Do staff members think about the occurrence of routine events and speculate on what might be the most likely causes of them and why? Or, is any thought given to the best actions to take for these and other events only when they occur?

All events are different and each requires a specific and appropriate management response to address the event and reduce the risk of triggering a crisis. Here in lies the dilemma: People in organizations can be so preoccupied with their own work that taking any time to think about what *might* happen does not have a place in their mindset. After all, how much time can be devoted to prepare for things that might never happen? The answer to this question is clearly one for the professional in the room.

Diagram 3.1 helps understand the nature of the event/crisis relationship and, by extension, what is at stake should a crisis emerge. This illustration introduces a truly dynamic assortment of occurrences needing to be addressed: an event, a crisis, a catastrophe and a disaster. It also points to ways a single event, crisis, catastrophe or disaster can unleash a myriad of ancillary issues someone must address. Whether taken in part or as a whole, it is a troubling state to consider.

The Description

Diagram 3.1 represents a stream of phenomena.[2] First we see that an EVENT occurs as the initial incident. Then, if circumstances surrounding the event are mismanaged, neglected or generally unaddressed a TRANSITIONAL state forms. This is a crucial point in the overall process reflected in the diagram as both the event and the transitional state must be managed. In other words, now those initially

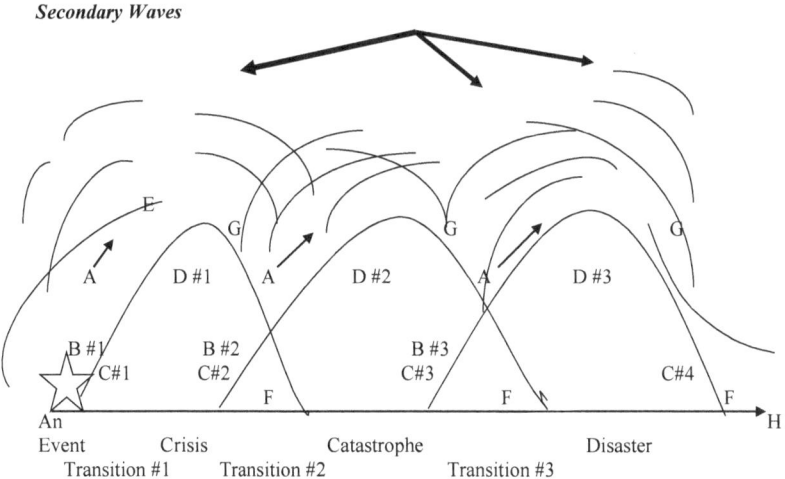

Secondary Waves

An
Event   Crisis   Catastrophe   Disaster
        Transition #1   Transition #2   Transition #3

KEY
A intensification of the phenomenon
B emergence of a new dynamic state (crisis, catastrophe or disaster)
C transition state from one phenomenon to the next
D new state is established
E loss of equilibrium
F effects continue
G declining intensification, Loss of Value
H timeline

Diagram 3.1 The phenom-stream: Sketching the wave processes from event to disaster

assigned to manage the event may find their resources thinned as they attempt to manage both the event and this new transitional state. Think back to our illustration of a fire. The fire is the initial event needing management but the transitional state can be defined by "evacuation events" or "notification events" for example of emergency services, "assessment events" associated with determining the severity of the fire and so on. The event sets the stage for the transition and the transition for whatever other event states that follow.

Next, in Diagram 3.1 we assume the EVENT (indicated by the "star") is not managed and the transition ("C#1") sets the stage for the EVENT to morph into a CRISIS. Once again, the stage is set for both effects of the crisis to trigger other, secondary events and for a second transition state ("C#2") to occur. What the organization's leadership must now recognize is that both the event and crisis have to be managed as well as transitional effects and effects spawned by the event and crisis.

For example, in Table 3.3 where a guest falls, that is the initial event. However if, in the management of the event, an attending nurse notices that with the fall the guest broke a leg bone and received some lacerations, both of these injuries need to be treated. These are effects spawned by the event, but if the fall happened at a nursing home that facility may not have the resources to treat the broken bone (e.g., take x-rays, set the bone, possibly operate on the leg) so a local hospital has to be notified. This means other stakeholders must be involved: an ambulance service, the family and, in some instances, local regulatory agencies that may be interested in circumstances associated with the fall. All of these become elements in the post-crisis transition phase. (Oh, and do not forget the attending nurse, who may get a back strain from trying to help raise the fallen person. That is yet another post-event effect needing attention.)

If circumstances associated with the crisis are not managed and the crisis is not contained (for example, the attending nurse did not believe the leg was broken when it was and simply treated abrasions) matters associated with the original fall take on a new profile. Not adequately addressing the fall allows the crisis to migrate into conditions related to the second TRANSITIONAL state, thus setting the stage for the crisis to morph into a catastrophe. Interestingly, too, this brings up an often overlooked but important part linked to the process that is unfolding and the role of these transitional states.

The event and crisis are obviously noteworthy, so data collection regarding the two is assumed. However, the transition states also are a rich source for information regarding both the overall process and what occurs between the event and crisis. For example, how much time passes between the event and emerging crisis? Who was involved during this period and why? Who was contacted and what information were they given? Who was not informed and why? What treatments were provided? Were drugs administered? What scheduled drugs were not administered, perhaps because in the confusion attending staff forgot to address this need? Any or all of these are additional circumstances initially may seem unrelated to the original event but they are if one looks at the overall process, and particularly as new stakeholders, like litigators or the media join the social network.

Transitions, then, are unique, rich sources for information and data but, importantly, their real value lies in understanding any role they play as one state morphs into a new state. When morphing occurs the second transitional state enables the crisis to morph into a CATASTROPHE. Here again, if mismanaged, this state can potentially move into the third TRANSITIONAL state and that, finally, into a DISASTER if mismanagement occurs or the previous state is NOT CONTAINED. There is little need to provide examples of Diagram 3.1. Just think of recent events and plug them into the model. Think, for example, of an airline crash, an oil spill, a politician's blunder or an executive charged with sexual abuse of an employee. They will all fit into the model and the relationship among these four phenomena will quickly become apparent.

Competency in Event Management and Crisis Containment Efforts

Chapter 4 provides a detailed examination of effects associated with a mismanaged event or crisis, catastrophe or disaster, and the costs associated with them. Now we are interested in reviewing one particular issue, the factors that contribute to poor performance in the face of potentially traumatic events or a more damaging crisis, catastrophe or disaster.

Several factors define both approaches to an event or crisis and results associated with any efforts extended. For example, broadly speaking, approaches can be preemptive or reactive, depending on the advance information available or the nature of the organization's culture. Preemptive approaches are anticipatory, with strategies that are blocking or preventative. Reactive approaches materialize after the event or crisis has occurred. Reactive strategies and tactics are problematic because hasty thinking and actions can affect them. These moves can be imprudent, even rash, as those attempting to address the phenomenon may simply toss anything at the event or crisis in the hopes that something will work.

Clearly, preemptive approaches are the ideal, but they may not be options for those involved. As a result, what we look at when examining responses to an event or crisis are the competencies and skills used when addressing them. In fact, here our basic premise is that crises emerge because of mismanaged events so the question for us to explore is why or how did mismanagement occur? To do this, our initial interest centers on the earliest moments of an event in order to model what may, or what has happened, and why.

As an introduction, Table 3.4 outlines a simple illustration for you to complete.

Now, whether you do this process on paper or just in your mind, when you complete the process you have established, at least for you, a baseline understanding of how you would address these three events. Next, if you have 3 or 4 others who work at your organization, have them complete the process. Then compare their responses to yours and, of course, their responses to each others.

Once these steps are complete, it is possible to ask several questions. For example, is there a best response for each event? What was the rationale behind the responses offered? For example, some might pass the event off to another to manage. What other information do you need? Another person might jump right in and take action. Why the differences?

Answers to these and other questions you might think of can be important; they can reveal a lot of information about how your staff might respond to relatively routine events and, importantly, how your organization as a whole might approach these and other, more extreme

Table 3.4 Developing baseline impressions of event response behavior

1. To begin this process study, here is a list of typical events that might occur in a nursing home or eldercare community

- Event #1: An employee trips and falls down the stairs, a distance of about ten feet. No other employees are around, just residents. You see this activity and do what?
- Event #2: After lunch three patients experience fevers, dizziness and nausea. One of them calls you, seeking help. So far you only know about these 3 experiencing symptoms, although more than 20 were fed. What do you do?
- Event #3: Accounts receivable receives a call from a patient who complains about the co-payment he paid after his last visit. He just received a letter saying he had not paid the co-payment and must do so now. He says he paid in cash but has a receipt. The Accounts Payable clerk asks for a copy of the receipt. The AP clerk treats it as a "done deal". You happen to hear about it from a friend who knows the patient. What do you do?

2. Next, for each event, complete what we call an "A to Z" process. To do this, list from start to finish, what you believe is the best effective response to manage each event.

3. Last step. Seek out 3 or 4 employees and give them the same three scenarios. Once they are finished, compare the responses.

events. Most importantly, we believe this information is especially critical because the mismanagement of an event is the primary predictor of why a crisis is triggered, so there is real value in understanding the range of factors that may have contributed to a crisis that your organization experiences. (Oh, and by the way, these are real events.)

Organization Capabilities and Capacity to Manage Events

Completing tasks like the example described in Table 3.4 is a way to introduce you to two important elements associated with your organization: the staffs' capability to approach and handle different events and the organization's overall capacity to perform when exposed to potentially risky events. These types of exercises provide a way to understand how staff might handle near-term events while providing a means for estimating how staff and those in the organization as a whole will perform if a crisis emerges. Then, of course, the issue to explore is how the staff might undertake efforts to contain the crisis if it emerges.

The next chapter delves into exposures and potential costs associated with poor performance. The remainder of this chapter continues with our discussion of factors associated with poor performance by dealing with issues associated with professional competencies and then matters associated with the types of action taken when faced with a threatening event or crisis. The bottom line for this discussion: the capability to act and the capacity to act *are not the same* but having both is *a must and not an option.*

Organizational readiness requires an examination that goes deeper than a review of staff skills and competencies associated with their personal jobs or assignments. Capacity is a potentially multidimensional construct. On one hand, individual and organizational capacity reflects the physical, cognitive and emotional ability, the means, to accomplish tasks, and to perform given the organization's needs. Beyond the capacity to handle a task or assignment are the *orientations* one brings to the organization and its efforts. In what ways do individual, departments, or the organizational as a whole approach the work and/or challenges they encounter?

Capabilities are unique because in addition to reflecting the potential to accomplish a mission, goals or objectives, capability also links back to aptitude and competence. It is not a "full circle" link but a process relationship. Capability is a means for understanding how the organization became the entity it is today and how it will perform tomorrow. Importantly too, it is a means for knowing how the organization can transition into something more, particularly when challenged by emerging threats.

The prepared organization is one that has both the capability and capacity to manage emerging challenges triggered by an event and/or crisis. We gauge the blend of capabilities and the capacity to perform in terms of three broad organizational dimensions.

- At the **macro, structural level**, three features define the organization's fitness: its architecture, its operations and its brand, the latter defining the organization for internal and external stakeholders. These three components provide a framework for organizational activity and image within its social networks.

- Next, at a **process level** a collection of key operational practices offer prescriptive expectations for what and how performance should occur. Table 2.2 in the previous chapter illustrated these key practices and ways they may shape an individual's performance. These practices appear throughout this book; they are embedded in performance management efforts and activities. Operational practices are reviewed here for a second reason, because the management of events or containment strategies used to successfully address crises, catastrophes and disasters must address both the physical nature of these phenomena as well as threats, weaknesses and vulnerabilities associated with or resulting from them. Well established operational practices are routes and boundaries for performance regardless of the setting or challenge.

- **Individual competencies** are the last area contributing to organizational performance. There are various ways to demonstrate the potential role of personal competencies in defining successful performance with routine and extreme tasks. Observations of performance and tests are examples. However, competencies can make their contribution to an organization's strengths if they are maintained and regularly evaluated. Failure to ensure these two requirements is a prescription for trouble.

Table 3.5 has examples of individual competencies and ways they reflect an organization's capabilities. Once in an organization, the individual agrees to perform and interact for a common good as expressed in the pursuit of the organization's vision and mission. Expected competencies link to one's occupation, job or assignment, and carry over to all opportunities an individual might have in the performance of tasks or assignments. In other words, the categories are not binding or delimiting but are rather both generic and pervasive throughout the organization and an individual's interactions and work.

The organization's structural elements and operational processes mesh with individual and organizational competencies to define the organization's strengths, weaknesses and vulnerabilities. In practice, individuals

Table 3.5 Competency and event management and crisis containment

Professional competencies

Professionalism exhibited	**Professionalism in application**
Occupational credentials	Program design
Content area proficiencies	Problem Identification/solving skills
Trade knowledge and practices	Knowledge (general & specific)
Evaluation and assessment skills	Experience in content areas
Branded and influential	Ability to create a "learning environment"
Administrative competencies	*Basic skills competencies*
Planning and goal setting	Use of training tools and techniques
Assessment skills	Ability to manage criticism
Time management	Speaking skills (e.g., use of examples)
Project management	Facilitation skills
Logistical skills	Presentation skills
Meeting management	Evaluation and assessment
Cultural awareness competencies	*Interpersonal/team competencies*
Political, economic & historical referents	Communication
Organizational climate and characteristics	Collaboration skills
Religious tolerances and expression	Mission awareness and focus
Rituals and customs, norms and mores	Listening
Social, recreational values and significance	Other orientations
Health, safety and security values	Sharing and involvement efforts
Arts, literature, music	

demonstrate their competencies in performance that contributes to the organization's strengths while reducing weaknesses and vulnerabilities. This enables individuals to function, given the organization's structure and operational processes, in ways to pursue the best courses of action to meet the needs, wants and desires of the organization's social order and stakeholders.

The Strategic and Tactical Make-up of What Occurred or Should Have but Did not and *Why*

It is clear that some approaches to event management or crisis containment occur without much regard for planning or even careful thinking; maybe there is just not time. This is not an orientation we subscribe to regardless of the nature of the event or crisis. We believe this for several reasons. First, if the organization has taken the time to recruit and train the right people then the staff should be available with the competencies to manage most events, even if this means drawing in outside resources to support the effort. Second, if the organization has built support systems within which staff can operate then the needed architecture is there from which to function. Finally, if the first two features operate within sound processes, procedures and practices then, again, management of a troublesome event should be within the organization's capability and capacity to handle.

This brings us to the event or crisis. Having the organization's staff and foundation in place is a great starting point but every event and crisis is different so organizing a plan is the next step in the process. There are many approaches to consider when addressing an event or crisis but here are five that can provide guidance or at least serve as a good starting point.

- First, it is important to know and understand the background for the event. Typical data points include what happened, who is involved and to what extent.
- Second, what choices do you have to act? If someone is injured can they be moved, if the building is on fire is the fire manageable and within the staffs' competencies and training? How much time do you have, or is this is life-threatening emergency that demands action now? In other words, consider the features of the event that define and shape how you can proceed.

- Third, make decisions and define your initial strategies and tactics. If the event is an obvious emergency, there is no need to build an elaborate plan with layers of strategic and tactical choices. Use a simple rule: event plus common sense equals action (for now). Here your strategy can start at the top: who is or should be involved and notified. If you can handle the situation, that is the first action-based decision. If someone is injured, has trouble breathing or is bleeding then those conditions guide your first actions. Just remember, to make the best decisions means you have access to information about the event, requirements needed to manage the event and, who is best to have take charge of the event. This is not an avoidance move or a "pass off" this is delegation of the event to the best person for the job.
- Fourth, take action. Know who is involved and why. What are your expectations for them and for all involved stakeholders? What is your communication plan? Who are the targets for your communications? What data or information do you need to monitor throughout the process? How are you doing for time? What contingencies are in place if the action falters or is not sufficient to manage the event? What are the next steps if the event morphs into a crisis?
- Fifth, observe, document and evaluate everything throughout and certainly after the overall process. There are practical reasons for this continual observation, documentation and evaluation effort. For example, observe and evaluate to make sure things are going well. Is there a need for more resources or are time constraints emerging? Make sure what is done is adding value, doing no harm. Observe and evaluate to ensure you have all relevant materials and information needed after managing the event or, worse, if it morphs into a crisis. And, finally, documentation and evaluations may be especially important should regulators or litigators join the social network.

Strategies and Tactics When Pressed into Action

The reasons for the fifth step should be straightforward but some miss this point. What, for example, might you or other researchers look for, or be prepared to act on, if there is a problem? To answer that question here are five indicators to examine when trying to see if performance and/or organizational issues may have compromised the event management process.

A first point is linked to the fundamental competencies of those charged with, or assuming, action in the event. Was taking action within the skills or competencies of the person taking action or leading the effort? Several variables can help you decide if there was a problem here for this individual. For example, did the individual (or group) avoid doing something that could have been or should have been done? Were key people who might have been involved overlooked? For example, if it was a medical emergency, was a doctor contacted in a timely manner? If it was a fire, was the fire department or police contacted immediately? Were requests made for their assistance in any way?

Is communication evident? Are key people informed or, if necessary, involved? Were those in senior management consistently informed regarding progress on the interventions? Are those involved working from the plan prescribed or any plan for that matter? Are things occurring in a timely manner? Are priorities getting addressed and, importantly, are the highest priority matters being addressed before lower priority issues? Are there any signs that tough issues or part of the job are avoided or, worse, skipped altogether? How do you know? What documentation exists regarding actions taken and the intervention overall.

2. *Any signs of competency shortcomings in the face of the event?* Given the competencies and skills outlined in Table 3.5, have you noticed or heard of any competency shortcomings? A troublesome event or crisis is not necessarily something most managers receive training and preparation for before they occur. So have you seen instances when someone who typically displayed strong leadership skills and judgment failed to display the same for this project? For example, is someone who was a good communicator in the past now missing opportunities to keep people informed or avoiding some people altogether? If you noticed this behavior, when did it come to your attention? Were involved staff overwhelmed? Was the support they needed for both project management and logistics available in a timely manner? What data do you have to support this?

Was the project's leadership suitably prepared for this event or crisis? How do you know? What materials do you have that supports your conclusions? Did the leader of this change effort appear to fold under pressures associated with the project or with particular tasks? Have you noticed any lack of clarity or confusion on the part of anyone associated with the effort? Do you feel everyone involved as a clear notion regarding the project's mission? The projects needs? The timeline? What data do you have to support this?

Did this event management effort require a wide array of skills and competencies and, if so, did the team or key people possess these skills? For example, medical events require special competencies so it is important to insure that someone with the needed background is part of the team or at least available. Does anyone on the team need to be replaced now or for future projects? How do you justify this conclusion?

Referring again to Table 3.5, have you noticed deficiencies in any basic skills like meeting management, planning or organizing? Are regular and ongoing assessments being conducted? Who gets the data from these assessments and with what results? Are team requests being met? Is it clear that they are getting the resources and information needed to act? Are there any budgetary matters interfering with their efforts? How do you know?

3. *What can you say about decisions made during the event?* Are risky decisions or actions taken without proper care? Is it clear those involved are thinking before they act? How do you know? Are any risky decisions or actions being avoided? Were criteria defining risk levels defined before beginning the intervention? How do you know? Are bureaucracy issues bogging down people or the team? Any examples? Are decisions made in a timely manner? Are key leaders/administrators making themselves available? Who is not but should be? Which leaders/administrators are doing a great job? Are things, decisions, actions being delegated that should not be? Is the team being asked to handle matters that should be handled by leadership or administrators? By outside agencies? Is the team getting all of the support it needs from the social network? Does the social network demonstrate and share the same sense of urgency for this project?

4. *In what ways did the Event/Crisis effect the possibility for solutions?* There are many ways to approach solutions for an event or crisis. The first, when the event is addressed early as a relatively discrete phenomenon and any solutions may be relatively straightforward. However, complex events, or events that spawn a number of sub-events, may require significant planning and preparation for multiple potential solutions.

Diagram 3.2 illustrates the second situation. It is a simple model but it conveys a lot of information. Here solutions offered have to be designed to manage the sub-events given (a) their priority or seriousness (b) any critical time factors, (c) the need for extra resources (e.g., specialists and, of course, (d) any organizational issues like "turf claims," leadership challenges, procedural disputes and the like. So, what looked like a relatively neat single event is now, given other considerations, a potential mess. Oh, and by the way, it looks like the original event or any of the sub-events might also morph into a crisis, yet another matter for the organization's leadership to navigate.

In fact, there may be matters associated with the event or the event itself where no solutions are possible. "Death" is an example. When a death occurs, there are ancillary details to manage (who, what, where, when, why or how) but no real solution for the initial event is possible.

Unless … of course, even death has a way of seemingly reformatting the original event. In situations like this, we begin by asking why the death occurred? If, for example, it was associated with a disease were others exposed and contaminated? Or, if the death was associated with another matter is that "matter" the REAL event needing a solution? Now, as a clearer picture materializes: the organization's leadership

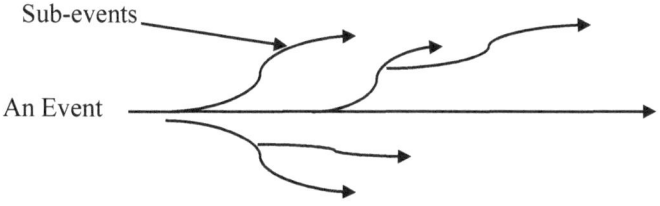

Diagram 3.2 An illustration of an initial event and spawned sub-events

may find they are dealing with yet another model like that portrayed in Diagram 3.2.

5. *Is it possible to delay action or to transfer the matter to someone else?* Then there are those instances when it is not necessary to address the Event/Crisis now. Perhaps it is a low-priority event or one that can be tabled until more people or financial resources are available. This is an important decision, however, that should be grounded in facts and real, meaningful data. Many a career has ended because an event was worked around as "not an issue" or left because of missing or poor information. If the matter clearly should be transferred to others or another organization then involve those stakeholders fast, as early as possible. Avoid waiting to see if what you have at your disposal might work, put the experts in charge and *manage them.*

This last point also is interesting because it brings us back to an earlier point when we began this section, and that has to do with the decisions on how to proceed when an event (or crisis) emerges. The decision to act is one thing but how to react is a separate matter altogether. Deciding how to react means those taking action are stipulating the strategies and tactics needed to manage the event. It also means that those defining the strategy and tactics know what needs to be done, who should be involved, what time issues are critical and so on. Remember, the STRATEGY IS NOT THE PLAN!

Conclusion

A strategy is a collection of tactics. In the broadest sense, the strategy is a statement regarding a possible set of actions that may meet an objective. This is a significant statement for it implies a greater understanding of leadership fundamentals associated with planning, organizing, managing and evaluating people, processes and organizations. For example, since the objective defines the strategy that means there are more than a few things at work when approaching a solution for an event.

Consider the flow outlined in Table 3.6. Just like for the organization as a whole, addressing an event begins with a vision regarding what needs to be/must be done. From that point, all else proceeds with each element

Table 3.6 How event management strategies evolve (and work)

How Event Management Strategies Evolve (and Work)
There is a **Vision** regarding what must be achieved regarding the Event
↓
That the Vision defines the **Mission** for the Event Management
↓
That the Mission helps define certain **Goals** for successful management (for example, for Safety, Security, Cost and the like)
↓
And that **Objectives** are emerge from the stipulated goals
↓
Activities aimed at achieving these objectives result in performance

clearly (and ideally quantitatively) defined. Moreover, screw up any point in this process and failure may be inevitable. Or, given the thrust of this book, there is potential for the event to morph into a crisis.

The following chapter closely examines details associated with effects of events and crises on organizations and their stakeholders. That analysis illustrates exposures healthcare organizations face when an event is mismanaged or morphs into a crisis, catastrophe or disaster. More importantly, it will demonstrate how items sketched in Diagrams 3.1 and 3.2 materialize to affect organizations facing these dilemmas. To this point, we can present the material covered as ways organizations in the face of an event or crisis struggle to deal with their circumstances. In the next chapter readers can come to grips with a worst-case scenario—a situation when part or all of an organization's systems face collapse. Plans resulting from the process outlined in Table 3.6 are scripts guiding those involved in the remediation effort with the *hows* to do something. As an end, plans are easy to construct; that does not mean they are easy to implement nor should they be sketched on a napkin!

Notes

1. Tafoya, Dennis. *The Effective Organization.* New York: Routledge, 2010, p. 138.
2. Tafoya, Dennis. *Crisis, Catastrophe, and Disaster in Organizations: Managing Threats to Operations, Architecture, Brand and Stakeholders.* New York: Palgrave/Macmillan, 2020, p. 80.

4

Products, Outcomes and Impacts of Events, Crises, Catastrophes and Disasters

Abstract It is easy to slip into the hype associated with an event or crisis. There is drama, there is action and there are opportunities for individuals to demonstrate their full range of competencies. However, at the same time, it is important to recognize that with all events and crises there are consequences; these phenomena are real, meaningful and can contribute to an organization's ultimate collapse. This chapter covers material needed to understand an organization's capabilities for managing troublesome events and/or containing a crisis, catastrophe or disaster.

Keyword Systems theory as a forensic tool · Building an organization's profile · Organizational Alignment

Introduction: It is easy to slip into the hype associated with an event or crisis. There is drama, there is action and there are opportunities for individuals to demonstrate their full range of competencies. However, at the same time, it is important to recognize that with all events and crises there are consequences; these phenomena are real, meaningful

D. W. Tafoya and L. Poeth, *Healthcare Leadership in Times of Crisis*, https://doi.org/10.1007/978-3-030-75965-0_4

and can contribute to an organization's ultimate collapse. This chapter covers material needed to understand an organization's capabilities for managing troublesome events and/or containing a crisis, catastrophe or disaster. To accomplish these objectives, it is important to understand the nature of the organization experiencing the event or crisis so that its strengths can be used to its advantage, and its weaknesses and vulnerabilities managed. Systems theory provides some answers but, in addition, systems theory also makes a unique contribution to a particular conundrum. It helps understand why healthcare organizations so familiar with the treatment of events and crises of others, so often fail when the crisis is of their own doing and effects their own organization.

A Systemic Orientation to Organizations, Their Stakeholders and Events, Crises, Catastrophes and Disasters

Systems theory is a useful approach to use when examining organizations. In fact, it is particularly useful when preparing a holistic image of an organization. We use it here, too, with a couple of notable exceptions. First, we tailor its use to organizations in the healthcare industry. Unlike organizations in other industries, the primary "customers" or clients for those in the healthcare industry can become temporary residents in these organization's facilities. They are not transient individuals who show up when they want to buy something at a store or restaurant and leave after a brief transaction or even a school where the students can leave at the end of a day. Most healthcare organization patients may remain in these organizations until they heal or, worse, they die. It is a feature that makes these organizations unique.

Second, our approach to the use of systems theory among healthcare organizations is unique as a tool in ways it helps our understanding of the role mismanaged troublesome events and crises play in any organization. In this instance, we demonstrate that while these healthcare organizations, given the nature of their business, should be models of the management of troublesome events or crises, they are not. Management of troublesome events and containment of crises is part of a healthcare organization's business model; it is part of the operational make-up of healthcare systems. Yet, despite this characteristic they are not immune to or better at managing troublesome or extreme events; staff in these organizations are as likely to make mistakes that can trigger the emergence of a crisis.

Our use of systems theory in this instance contributes to our understanding of why performance associated with what otherwise should be familiar, normal events fails. The salient issue to explore here is that when an event is mismanaged and triggers a crisis in a healthcare organization what emerges is a dynamic tension between two "competing" systems. One system defined by the healthcare organization and the other defined by the very crisis spawned through event mismanagement.

In these instances, healthcare organizations experience a condition observed in organizations in other industries. Once a traumatic event or crisis emerges for an organization the "systemic crisis" engages with the organization's systemic nature and the two systems become "part" of each other. A relationship forms between the self-created troublesome event or emerging crisis and the organization because, it is in the nature of systems to influence and generates change in phenomena associated with them. The emerging systems spawned by mismanaged events and subsequent crises stimulate the creation of products, outcomes and impacts that can so dominate the organization's system it can fail. Likewise, to further muddy the dynamic circumstances emerging with a mismanaged event or triggered crisis is the activity of the organization's staff. Those engaged in event management or crisis containment efforts generate their own sets of products, outcomes and impacts as solutions for containing the crisis, thus producing meta systems to compete with the event or crisis systems and the organization's own systemic nature.

Finally, and importantly, as these systems come in contact with each other, the effects they spawn are not localized but can influence the overall nature of everything and everyone involved in the management or containment effort. In short, the systemic nature of a mismanaged event or emerging crisis affects and simultaneously demands the attention of all stakeholders in the organization's social network. The surgery event that leads to a patient's death spawns events that spread throughout the organization. Impact to the organization's brand as a surgery center touches the business model. Threats of litigation generate meetings throughout operations as staff explore materials and equipment, procedures and processes and skills and competencies to help them in their efforts. And these are just the circumstances associated with one event that happened on one day in one surgery.

An Introduction to the Use of Systems Theory as a Forensic Tool

Using a systemic framework to examine events and crises as part of the healthcare center can help us understand how and why negative conditions related to an event or crisis have the effects they do. System thinking is a useful forensic tool when diagnosing a problem and building strategies and tactics to address emerging issues and challenges. Toward that end, the material that follows is organized around examples of ways systems theory can be tailored for use as a research tool.

Using systems theory as a forensic tool begins with a brief review of the nature of the target organization. The objective is to gain insight into the structural make-up of the organization. This provides an overview of strengths and weaknesses within the fabric of the organization. Weaknesses point to potential vulnerabilities and risks should threats imposed by troublesome events or crises arise. The organization's strengths reveal opportunities for countering weaknesses or vulnerabilities so knowledge of all of these elements is valuable.

Matching strengths to weaknesses or vulnerabilities is not a simple, linear process however. People affiliate with organizations because they believe the organization will deliver services or products the individual cannot deliver themselves; it is a personal choice. When the individual's choice involves a healthcare organization, the choice reflects healthcare and a lifestyle needs, wants and desires. These are deep-seated pursuits and can reveal the manner in which organizations seek to identify and meet stakeholder needs through the products and services they offer and the image they construct through their brand. This is an important feature to understand because it illustrates how organizations use their image, their brand, to get stakeholders to buy into the products and services offered. This becomes a "promise" bent on fulfillment of the stakeholder's needs: "you have these needs, wants and desires and this is how we will meet them through our products and services." Herein, then, is where the organization's business model is rooted in performance and why mismanagement of even a routine event can challenge the organization's capacity to meet this obligation.

Once made (or implied) promises regarding the fulfillment of personal needs means the organization must deliver on those promises. Organizations do this through their structural make-up as well as their products and services. The organization's architecture, operations and brand or image become pathways for the organization's stakeholders to believe that personal needs, wants and desires can be fulfilled by the organization. Troublesome events or crises threaten these pathways creating the potential for disruptions to interfere with the organization's ability to fulfill its obligations. Moreover, with these disruptions come increasing risk exposures, added vulnerabilities and potential damage to reputations and image.

When threats and crises emerge, the organization's leadership and stakeholders begin to understand the array of risks they face. Ironically, tracing emerging threats reveal dangers associated with the events and crises and the capacity of the organization staff to respond. Now those in leadership positions have an opportunity to see that external dangers can magnify if combined with internal shortcomings. It also is an excellent point at which the organization's leadership can begin to think about ways the interactions different systems are contributing to a range of negative, damaging effects associated not only with the event or crisis but also with efforts associated with event management or crisis containment efforts. It is a classic dilemma many face in healthcare delivery have experienced when the prescribed treatment is a potentially damaging as the issue it is designed to address.

We start the chapter by looking at elements of an organization's profile as a good place to begin when thinking about a response plan for the challenges faced. No individual, group or organization is completely without resources but recognizing these capabilities is not always evident when challenges or threats seem to overwhelm those launching the change effort. Fear can grip those faced with a crisis if they lose sight of their strengths and capabilities. Learning how to identify one's resources available in times of stress and trouble is a solid leadership trait. Finally, the chapter ends with suggestions on how stakeholders can match what they know and learn how to build an effective response plan.

Using Systems Theory to Build an Organizational Profile

The model in Table 4.1 is useful when examining any type of organization, but our focus centers on healthcare organizations with managed care capabilities. Material in the table summarizes information presented earlier but here the focus is on systemic performance in a well-designed healthcare center. This view in Table 4.1 pictures the organization prior to the emergence of a troublesome event or crisis and so assumes that should an event or crisis materialize organizations with this profile should be capable of managing the challenge but, at the same time, is susceptible to change.

Another perspective of the profile presented in Table 4.1 is that it is a baseline for healthcare delivery systems; it presents an ideal picture of what to see in a well-designed organization. It is a profile of what one would like to see in these organizations as they function to manage day-to-day activities in order to meet stakeholder needs.

A few questions illustrate the value when using this material as a template or guide. For example, think of a scenario where troublesome events like those discussed earlier in the book emerge and ask yourself what effects having a poorly trained staff might have on the event's management. Or, what if the materials or equipment needed to respond to a critical event are not available, for example, if there is insufficient protective gear when faced with a virus? What if there is a lack of safety training for staff faced with a patient experiencing severe emotional stress associated with a injury or accident? The material sketched in Table 4.1 is a "high level" view of an effective organization yet it makes it possible to imagine what a more detailed template might look like for the truly proactive organization.

Table 4.1 An ideal healthcare organization's profile (Based on a summary of material presented in Table 2.1)

Assessment area	Representative performance criteria
People—Clients/Patients	• Receiving prescribed care
	• Receiving prescribed medication
	• Living in a safe environment to avoid accidents or injury
	• Having Personal and Social Needs Met
People—Administration	• Experienced administrators with healthcare/management backgrounds
	• Skilled in timely problem or issue management
	• Hands on professionals able to handle personnel matters
People—Staffing	• Vetted individuals working through performance management programs
	• Skilled with appropriate training and certifications
	• Targeted performance levels that "meet" or "exceed" expectations
	• Stable work environments with reduced or managed turnover
	• Exceptional performance during emergencies
Processes: How they work	• Safety programs in place and evaluated
	• Quality programs in place and evaluated
	• Security programs in place and evaluated
	• Customer service programs in place and evaluated
	• Operational practices, procedures in place and evaluated
Material needs	• Needed materials in place and evaluated
	• Materials for special needs in place and evaluated
	• Inventory processes in place for goods and materials
Equipment & Facility needs	• Appropriate equipment in place
	• Regular maintenance programs in place for key equipment
	• Operators trained and certified for safe equipment operations

(continued)

Table 4.1   (continued)

Assessment area	Representative performance criteria
Financing	• Annual budgets in place
	• Budgeted lines for operations improvements
	• Budgeted lines for emergencies or unexpected needs
Rules & Regulations	• Rules and regulations are defined and followed
	• Part of new hire training and orientation
	• Timely management of infractions
	• Regular review of rules and regulations
Organizational Culture	• Supportive organizational culture
	• Culture supports communication and collaboration
	• Culture supports fairness and objectivity
	• A safe, hostility-free environment

There are major differences between organizations and that is to be expected but the information in Table 4.1 reminds us that there are fundamentals to look for in all organizations. The prudent leader or manager can build off this generic guide so that it reflects the particular nature of his or her own organization. For example, it is easy to see how as a guide it is possible to specify quantitative performance indicators for key areas in the table or to build plans and programs to achieve particular objectives within each assessment area. In this manner, the template becomes a guide that allows for the evaluation of performance for specific departments or the overall organization.

Finally, if using this or a similar template reveals vulnerabilities or risks within the organization, knowing where weaknesses are makes it possible to address them before the emergence of a troublesome event. Alternatively, even if some event emerges in the meantime, those in the organization know where they may be most vulnerable to the event's effects or where existing deficiencies may hinder effective management efforts. The extent of damage may be significant in vulnerable areas but, at the same time, at least those involved at leadership levels will have a better idea why and how their organization and staff failed to meet the challenges brought on by the event.

Examining the Organization's Systemic Draw: When Organizations Design Promises to Meet Stakeholder Needs, Wants and Desires

Marketing professionals have learned that three characteristics make healthcare organizations different from most other organizations. First, people who join the social networks of these organizations as patients tend to have a long-term relationship with the organization. Theirs is not a transient relationship like the relationship experienced by people who float in and out of retail organizations, schools or even religions. Joining the membership roles of a healthcare organization signals a change in one's approach to health and life; it is recognition that there are limits to what one can do for one's self. It is a willingness to extend one's care, custody and control to others. And, it's a measure of trust.

Associated with this first feature is a second: Restrictions regarding the freedom to move about as one wants may be significant with the occurrence of dramatic changes in one's lifestyle. Patients extend authority over their behavior to healthcare providers with the understanding that these professionals act and behave with their best interests in mind. This is a much a psychological action on the patient's part as it is a physical move.

Finally, healthcare organizations are, in fact, healthcare delivery systems. Information drives these systems. Interviews, tests and audits establish a patient's health and medical needs on entry so that plans and actions needed to support their health and well-being are prepared, monitored and serviced. Then, as healthcare needs change or emerge, appropriate healthcare providers, the doctors, nurses, physical therapists or whatever can be made available to meet current or developing needs.

What is most unique about this point is the interaction that patients and healthcare staff mutually agreed upon in this new, "multi-dependent relationship." Nursing homes are a good example of this phenomenon. Residents relinquish certain rights and privileges as a prerequisite for joining the organization and the organization pledges the resources needed to meet the resident's needs. It is an important point because by agreeing to accept responsibility for the patient's care, custody and control the organization must be prepared to manage any troublesome event or crisis that emerges to threaten this relationship.

When an event or crisis does threaten operations, patients and the organization are exposed to different potential threats, conceivably requiring different action plans. For example, consider how representative baseline conditions may change. Healthcare services for individuals who require significant medical care, such as a ventilator, respiratory therapy, continuous or IV medications, and/or have higher level (stage 3+) wounds needing care cannot experience significant disruption of service. These conditions define boundaries or limitations associated with the type and delivery of healthcare required. The emergence of a troublesome event or crisis can disrupt "normal" conditions and potentially threaten the patient's well-being if tragedy emerges. The COVID-19 pandemic illustrates this type of threat. As the need for ventilators for individuals suffering from the virus increased, some hospitals found these in short supply. A first response is to look inside the organization to see what ventilator resources are available. What effect does this have on the organization whose existing patients already rely exhaused the existing supply of these machines?

Understanding the Subtle, Additional Issues—Otherwise Known as the "Particulars"

Inherent in the nature of healthcare organizations is the fact that they service a range of individuals, some of whom may already be in a legal, protected class. So, the fact that these patients are already in a documented legal protected class, establishes an a priori level of risk exposure and vulnerability for the organizations *before* the emergence of a troublesome event or crisis.

Next when a healthcare organization experiences a disruptive event or crisis, these events can have two different levels of impact on some patients. There is the chaos that effects all stakeholders (e.g., there's a fire and the building must be evacuated) and there are the effects that are specific to a given individual (e.g., the individual needs to be attached to a ventilator and moving that machine with the resident may be difficult given its location during the fire evacuation). So some individuals face multiple levels of risk from the same event or crisis.

Finally, with all of the potential stresses, strains and turmoil, that need managing in the face of a threatening event or crisis it is important to keep in mind that the needs, wants and desires of stakeholders within and outside the organization do not go away just because of an impending event or crisis. In other words, crisis management means more than attending to the event or issue at hand; it requires simultaneous management of a very dynamic and diverse collection of systems defining the healthcare delivery process.

Diagram 4.1 captures a simple view of part of that diverse system. We know there is a patient and, ok family members too, but what about friends and the patient's extended "support services." Lawyers, media and competing healthcare services can surface for any patient at any time to become part of the system. Diagram 4.1 is a simple view but it provides a fuller view of the healthcare organization's potentially fuller relationship with the client and, importantly, the client's complete stakeholder mix.

In actuality when the organization, whether hospitals or general healthcare services present their products, services (and promises) to a prospective mix of friends, family members and the patient they also are "presenting them" to a collection of "discovered" stakeholders. When a crisis breaks expect to see more than just the patient. Any healthcare

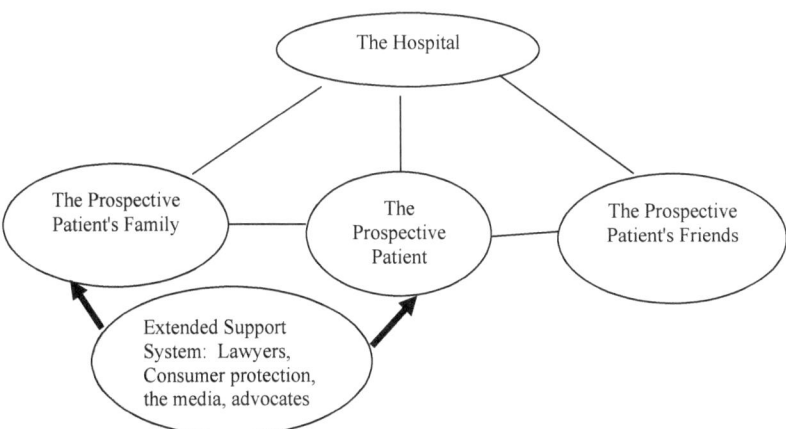

Diagram 4.1   A simple view of a prospective patient's (extended) stakeholder network

organization seeking to develop a relationship with a patient must recognize that the prospective patient links to a unique slate of "influencers" and with their own mix of known and unknown needs.

Identifying a Resident's Needs, Wants and Desires: A Tool Approach

Some of the material and discussion points covered to this point in the chapter may seem eccentric to those who read this book in search of tools for managing trouble events, preventing the triggering of a crisis or containing the crisis once it materializes. Yet, this material is critical to discuss because if we want to understand the complexities associated with a troublesome event, a crisis and an organization's potential response it is important to keep in mind any stakeholder's motivation for joining the organization.

This is particularly true when looking at healthcare organizations. Those who enter into a relationship with these organizations as patients recognize limitations in their own capacity for self-managed care; they are experiencing a unique lifetime transition. Relinquishing one's care to others occurs is a way for recognizing personal limitations and vulnerabilities. Everyone involved in leading, managing and working in organizations with a healthcare focus need to incorporate this material into their behavioral and mental mindsets.

One of the best ways to identify stakeholder needs is to ask questions tailored to get this information. In this instance, the central focus of these surveys centers around ways to identify lifestyle and healthcare needs in the broadest sense; it is a process for building a database of needs to meet current and, potentially, future events.

Brainstorming sessions are an example of a straightforward approach. In these instances the stakeholders simply tell you their needs as they come to mind. Once collected a next step in the process is to transfer the needs expressed with a scale to so the stakeholder can rate each need. This provides a measure of each need's intensity or importance. This paperwork is then given back to the stakeholders so they have a record of the ratings for each potential need. Finally, now both the practitioner and patient have quantitative data for immediate use or for use when meeting with others.

It is important to note here that there are two reasons why we refer to "stakeholders" and not just the prospective resident for this process. The first, is that it often is helpful to get a big picture of how the family, the prospective patient and other key "stakeholders" feel since, in many instances, more than just the prospective patient is involved in decisions regarding future healthcare and lifestyle needs. Friends, neighbors, members of religious communities may have a prominent role in the lives of these individuals. The second reason for doing this type of analysis is that even if a number of people participate in the overall assessment, it is easy to examine the ratings of particular individuals to gain different insights into what individuals see as important needs for them, versus the overall perceptions of the group. The internet contains information to use when constructing this type of assessment.

The Organization's Systemic Delivery Mechanisms: The Organization's Architecture, Operations and the Brand

The nature of the bond between an individual and an organization's brand or image may contribute to the brand's flexibility under the pressures of a troublesome event or crisis but the organization's architecture and operations are not as elastic. Some see an organization's architecture, its structure, as the foundation for the design, development and delivery of products and services. The architecture defines a mix of "hard" and "soft" concept elements, including both business functions and people needed to achieve its goals. This orientation can include suppliers, distribution, customers and employees.[1]

Others see the organizational architecture as "a description of the systems existing in the organization." They can be extremely formal or informal but they combine to describe the systems, which make the organization a living organization.[2] Two of the most notable approaches to describe an organizational architecture are Jay Galbraith's "Star Model™"[3] and the McKinsey consulting group's 7-S Framework.

In the Star Model™, organizational design policies fall into five categories. The first is *strategy*, which identifies the organization's direction over the next three to five years. The second is *structure*, which includes the arrangement and configuration of organizational units of responsibility. The third, *processes*, includes the overall flow of activity in the organization. The fourth point in Galbraith's star refers to the use of *rewards and reward systems* to motivate people. The fifth category of the model reflects *policies* that contribute to influencing performance. McKinsey's 7-S, is particularly unique because it offers "a framework introduced to address the critical role of coordination, rather than structure, in organizational effectiveness."[4]

Determining which model is best is a matter of choice. What is important to note, however, is that regardless of the model used an emerging event or crisis can wreak havoc by disrupting vulnerable architectural features. Whether tailoring a response to manage an event or to contain an emerging crisis, shifting organizational resources as a response to an event or crisis is disruptive. Shifted finances to cover costs associated with the event management or crisis containment effort may mean there are financial shortfalls later, other times the resources are people expected to stop what they are doing and to shift from regular duties to tackle the needs required by the impending event or crisis. Whatever the case, responding to an event or crisis directly affects the organization's operations and architecture.

In short, the organization responding to a threatening event or crisis can create additional problems for itself. The overriding point is that the mere emergence of a troublesome event disrupts normal routines. Even reactions to warnings of an approaching storm or hurricane, for example, influences behavior, whether the storm is an issue for the organization or not. Indeed, failure to take these warnings seriously may be just the type of irresponsible behavior that creates the shift from an "event-stage" to a "crisis-stage" for the organization.

Physical disruptions are only part of the effects triggered by an emerging or actual event or crisis, however. These physical effects are what we observe or may have learned to observe if, for example, the organization is located in an area where hurricanes or major storms occur. What those in affected organizations often do not see are ways in which the overall fabric of their organization changes, and sometimes is even damaged by events and crises.

Jonathan Trevor and Barry Varcoe[5] illustrate a very important point related to this issue in their article, "How Aligned is Your Organization?" The concept "organizational alignment" refers to the ordered nature of organizational elements that provide direction for the completion of tasks and activities. These elements need to be defined, integrated in conjunction with other elements and aligned for maximum benefit. According to Trevor and Varcoe, "Most executives today know their enterprises should be aligned. They know their strategies, organizational capabilities, resources and management systems should all be arranged to support the enterprise's purpose. The challenge is that executives tend to focus on one of these areas to the exclusion of the others, but what really matters for performance is how they all fit together. Consider their example using the fast food restaurant chain, McDonald's:

> What does it take to be able to serve over 1% of the world's population — more than 70 million customers — every day and in virtually every country across the world? Fanatical attention to the design and management of scalable processes, routines, and a working culture by which simple, stand-alone, and standardized products are sold globally at a predictable, and therefore manageable, volume, quality, and cost. Maximizing economies of scale lies at the heart of McDonald's product-centric business model. Efficiency is built into the design of its winning organization in the form of formalized hierarchies of performance accountability, a high division of labor, routinization of specialist tasks, and teamwork at the point of sale. McDonald's has been the market leader in its sector for decades.
>
> This is what enterprise alignment looks like. It means winning through a tightly managed enterprise value chain that connects an enterprise's *purpose* (what we do and why we do it) to its *business strategy* (what we are trying to win at to fulfill our purpose), *organizational capability*

(what we need to be good at to win), *resource architecture* (what makes us good), and, finally, *management systems* (what delivers the winning performance we need). The enterprise value chain is only as strong as its weakest link.[6]

Skilled healthcare organizations are experienced operations, but if their organizational alignment is compromised prior to a crisis or disrupted after one emerges then risk exposures can affect all stakeholders, physical property and operations. A conclusion to draw from Trevor and Varcoes' piece is that operations in the most experienced and sophisticated organizations, even a fast food organization like McDonald's, are exposed to potential disruptions with the emergence of a troublesome event or crisis. Poorly prepared food, a rude employee or a disagreeable customer for restaurants are not earth-shattering events, but they can have a negative impact on the organization's otherwise routine, smoothly functioning restaurant atmosphere.

Talking about alignment as an issue seems a straightforward point to consider, but take a minute and think about the elements that might define your organization and where alignment may be an important requirement before or after a crisis containment effort. Below are fifteen features common to most organizations. Features which one would expect should be both carefully defined and in strong alignment with the organization's vision, mission and operational features. Look over the table and assess your own organization's alignment. Finally, here is one thing to keep in mind as you review the information in Table 4.2: none of the items listed are "nice to have." In fact, one could build a case for these being representative of "organizational musts" for effective performance and operations.

Table 4.2 Tracing an organization's alignment on key operational features

Structural and Administrative Components	Operations	Processes and People
Planning and design Strategic planning Business planning Operations planning Marketing planning Social network planning	*Emergency management* Fire safety plans and designs Security plans and designs Safety plans and designs Quality plans and designs Environmental quality	*Administration* Line management Supervisor staff Special projects staff Overall training for all Overall certifications where needed Performance appraisals Disciplinary programs
Government relations Federal regulatory relations State regulatory relations Local regulatory relations State legislative relations Specifics for safety and health	*Plant and equipment* Maintenance programs and plans Operator training Operator certifications Safety guidelines Equipment statistics (age, usage) Property management and security	*Operations staff* Tasks and responsibilities defined Knowledge and skills defined Training in place Certifications where needed Performance appraisals Disciplinary programs Appropriate background checks
Local support relations Police relations Emergency management teams Hospital relations Medical support staff relations	*Communication and information processes and equipment* Cyber security plans and processes Staff training and certifications Department level trainings System upgrades	*Training and certification programs* Training and development programs Certification processes in place Evaluation programs Data management in place
Budgets and finance Overall budget planning Overall budgets in place Budgets by departments done Annual budget reviews	*Product and services design and development* Design planning Innovation method Evaluation procedures in place Safety processes	*Organization policies and procedures* Policies, procedures in place Annual audits Conformance plans Compensation plans and programs Incentives and rewards programs Safety and health programs

(continued)

Table 4.2 (continued)

Structural and Administrative Components	Operations	Processes and People
Customer and client relations	*Corporate culture*	*Operational processes by departments are defined*
Customer needs assessments	Performance standards	
Customer needs defined	Business ethics	Processes for productivity
Special needs defined	Fairness and civility	Processes for safety
Quality standards defined	Work ethics	Processes for quality
Service standards defined	Customer orientation	Processes for service
Identify and meet special		

The Contribution of the Organization's Brand in Efforts to Fulfill a Resident's Needs, Wants and Desires

An organization's brand anchors the organization's mission for stakeholders, whether for or against it. When a crisis emerges, the organization's brand is often most resilient to the dissonance associated with the crisis because of its personal link to the individual. Those in organizations often like to believe that they define the brand for its stakeholders, but while the brand may have certain public features (signage, themes or images) it is the individual stakeholder that constructs the brand's personal meaning and significance[7] (Tafoya 2018, 2020).

Brands are useful marketing tools when defining the difference between one organization and others. In some instances, the organization's brand is a way to add status to the individual's decision to pick one organization over another. Brands are often the roots for a "we vs they" mentality. In this capacity, brands can serve as a point of departure for action. The brand can serve as justification or rationale for what we do and how we do it. In this sense, the organization's brand is both a communication and marketing device. If the brand positions the healthcare organization as providing *the* state of the art medical care in the region this may be used to justify prices charged for treatments or services. It is a type of "you get what you pay for" approach.

Brands reflect and represent the organization's norms and values. In these instances, the brand serves as base for those seeking the organization's products and services while adding additional links to their relationship. In the end, this further cements patient's bond to the organization and the rationale for membership. "We can afford the best, so we go to the best."

On a day-to-day basis or when push comes to shove, organizational leaders use of the brand serves as a referent for decision-making and problem-solving. The brand is more than a guide in these instances; it literally helps us pick a course of action, what we want to do to demonstrate our position. In this capacity, the brand becomes a referent when assigning priorities to problems, to actions taken. It is the organization's leadership that has a way to tell staff members and stakeholders what to do 1st, 2nd and 3rd to make our points heard. In these instances, the organization's brand or image also becomes a means for justifying decisions, choices made or actions taken. Finally, like the first point made above, the brand is a benchmark against which stakeholders assess "how we performed" as well as "why" we performed as we did.

Addressing the Threats to the Organization: Using Systems Theory to Reveal the Emergence of Challenges Brought on by the Phenom Stream

Table 4.3 provides another view of what we refer to as "the Phenom Stream." The concept was presented in detail in Chapter 2 but this is a useful perspective here because studying the stream defining the relationship among events, crises, catastrophes and disasters allows the organization's leadership to drill into the potential for trauma with each point in the spectrum and, as such, reveal complexities associated with challenges facing those expected to manage the event or contain the crisis.

While we can learn from past experiences, each new event, crisis, catastrophe or disaster has to be valued in terms of its own systemic make-up. Gauging the systemic make-up of these phenomena is captured in two ways. First, we focus on three elements associated with the phenomena: the threats produced, the immediate risk exposures revealed and short- and long-term vulnerabilities either resulting from the event or crisis, or existing and magnified within the organization, thus contributing to potentially long lasting harm or damage[8] (Table 4.3).

Threats are meaningful, existing or potential phenomena that can negatively impact the organization. We do not usually think of threats as naturally occurring unless they are associated with some extreme event, like a raging wild fire or hurricane. Even in these cases, the threat does not emerge as with damaging potential because of the event, per se, but the staff's lack of preparation for it. This said, threats are best viewed as the products of stakeholders who may be adversaries or, in some instances, even unskilled or well-meaning members of the organization's staff. Threats to healthcare delivery services come from a variety of sources like competitors, regulators, disgruntled employees, litigators or again, well-intentioned friends or employees who act when they probably should not.

Risks are often associated with the organization or its business. Sometimes these risks describe a "cost of doing business" as when extra testing creates expenses associated with the monitoring or containment of a disease. Other risks are inherent with the nature of the business. Disease and infections are ever-present risks for those in healthcare services devoted to serving particular populations. Finally, there are risks triggered by secondary agents like lawyers and investigators whose businesses or professions are associated with responding to allegations of mismanagement or treatments that result in injury, disability or loss of life.

Risks can result in collapse of particular areas within the organization or in the extreme case, the organization itself. When risks result in emergence of a threat, or when they create the potential for vulnerabilities to arise, they are especially dangerous. An exposed risk sets up the prospect of a weakened organization that is vulnerable to attack, loss of market share or to the loss of its credibility or image.

Table 4.3 Forensics and the phenom spectrum: Illustrating ways events, crises and potential trauma might materialize in a healthcare organization

Level I—An event: A jam, pickle, fix, mishap – > mess, confusion, chaos, disorder, disarray. Scope: Typically, within the capacity of the organization to address.	Example: A fall results in a broken leg An issue with customer service A resident has a stroke A missed deadline A patient begins to wander around Patient has diarrhea	Trauma potential: Damage may occur but will likely be local, containable. Potential trauma damage: High, certainly local
Level II—A crisis: An impasse, problem, quandary > misfortune, adversity, hardship. Scope: Addressed in the organization in conjunction with some external assistance.	Example: A patient's cut is infected A positive test for COVID Key employee leaves Inappropriate behavior A patient has food poisoning	Trauma potential: Damage is possible. Potential Trauma Damage: Very High, within networks Potentially Wide Spread
Level III—A catastrophe: A debacle, cataclysm – > tragedy, blow, adversity, danger, deluge, wreckage. Scope: External assistance needed; organization must support	Example: Sexual harassment revealed Overcharging Medicaid A patient's death is covered-up Malpractice COVID outbreak spreads	Trauma potential: Damage and loss are probable, possibly extensive Potential trauma damage: Very high, wide spread
Level IV—A disaster: Real devastation, destruction – > calamity, ruin, upheaval, tragedy. Scope: External assistance required and leads the effort.	Example: Leader's unethical behavior Major fire with loss of life Patients with COVID-19 die	Trauma potential: Damage and loss are inevitable and likely extensive. Immediate action is required. Manage the effects and recovery. Reconsider future plans Potential trauma damage: Very high, wide spread

Vulnerabilities reflect a potential for the organization to suffer from or succumb to negative effects associated with events and/or crises, catastrophes or disasters. Vulnerabilities in healthcare organizations are most significant when they are associated with the organization's inherent nature, or the sheer nature of an event and/crisis. Measuring vulnerabilities in these instances focus on the potential for effects that contribute to damage or injury to the organization or its stakeholders.

These three states are unique in their own right as are their potential effects for an organization. However, it also is important to note that their effects can and do overlap. A threat that exposes or takes advantage of a vulnerability and which, in turn, may lead to damaging risk exposures for the organization, is troublesome on all three fronts. In these instances, the organization's leadership must launch activities to address the immediate issue in tandem with activities to mitigate effects of the threat, risks and vulnerabilities. In addition, challenges facing staff expected to intervene in these situations increase, potentially triggering other exposures. This is one reason why phenomena like a fire, the COVID-19 virus or the unchecked spread of bacterial infections are so problematic. Stakeholders not immediately associated with the event, like visitors or vendors, may find themselves swept up in phenomena that are not in any way directly related to them.

A takeaway from this discussion is that there are important ways the phenom stream combines and interacts with or contributes to the organizations susceptibility to threats, risks and vulnerabilities. Systemic analysis in these instances seek to isolate the particular and unique products, outcomes and impacts associated with each phenomenon and, at the same time, speculate on the risks, threats and vulnerabilities that may result. In the end, this analysis will set the stage for the design of plans to manage the events and/or contain the crises, catastrophes and disasters that emerge. It is an important point when documentation is especially critical for the development of a successful action plan.

The columns in Table 4.3 introduce and illustrate typical complexities we are interested in understanding and illustrate where and how documentation is important. The table is a unique way to sketch the nature of the phenomenon we are observing but, at the same time, material generated by its use hardly provides a complete picture of the full scope and scale of an event or crisis. For example, the middle column in Table 4.3 contains examples of each phenomenon but the astute reader will recognize that, upon close inspection, all of these examples are merely the tip of what may be part of a large iceberg in an ice flow composed of numerous icebergs.

Use the example in Level I as an illustration. What does "poor customer service" mean? A front-line worker dealing with a medical emergency may have one sense for what timely customer service means when shopping in a department store, but a very different sense when working with a patient. It also is important to look at the person charged with poor customer service. That person may not feel as though there was anything wrong with the service provided. "It's what I always do!"

And what about a missed deadline? Is missing the deadline the problem, or are ramifications associated with missing the deadline the real concern? Perhaps, it is the stakeholders involved in the deadline that is important. Responding to an attorney, a judge or, a federal regulator are obviously all different stakeholders, but each has a particular interest in their own deadlines, and all of them have a special interest if the missed deadline is associated with a case that involves *all of them*! So how can we get at the consequences associated with the phenomena? How can we begin to define the products, outcomes and impact of an event or crisis in order to launch an effective management or containment plan and strategy?

Real Time Results: Products, Outcomes and Impacts Across Stakeholders and the Organization

Three particular features define every event or crisis: First, events and crises generate *products* that may harm the organization. Next, the products produce a secondary effect labeled as an *outcome* and third, every outcome produces some *impact(s)* on the organization.[9] Diagram 4.2 presents a simple illustration of these features and their relationship. In the example, the fire does not have to be large for the range of products, outcomes and impacts associated to be significant.

The initial orientation to an event or emerging crisis focuses on the *products associated with the event*. These products are the *observable results*

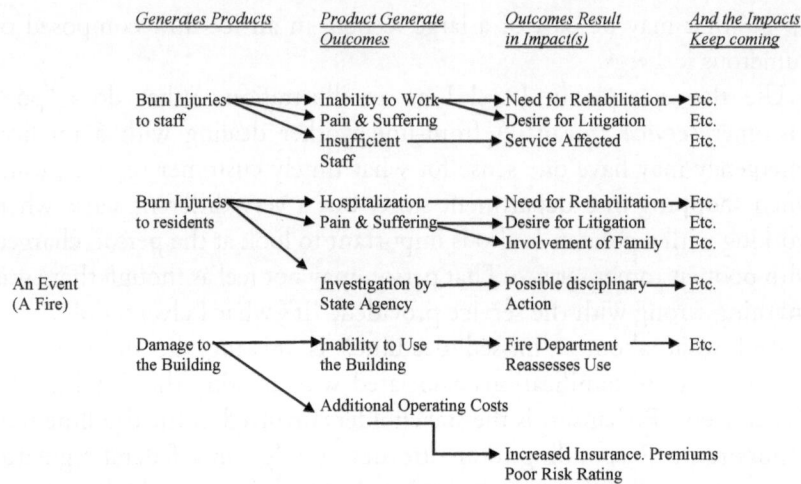

Diagram 4.2 The relationship between an event and products, outcomes and Impacts associated with it (Example: A fire in a skilled nursing facility)

or consequences associated with the event or crisis. In our fire example, a product might be a burn injury, or flame and smoke damage. Products may be tangible or intangible, the emotions and fear associated with activity and effort as people flee the fire. *Products reflect three things*: First, an organization's or an individual's desires or needs, as often reflected in a mission, philosophy, ideology or values. You see a fire, do something; put it out or call someone to put it out. Actions here often reflect part of the organization's culture or make-up; its orientation to action.

Second, products are directly associated with activity, capability, capacity or competency. If it is a small fire and you have the tools (e.g., a fire extinguisher), put it out. Products require a response and the adequacy of the response provided reflects the organizations or individuals' capabilities or competencies. Third, products reflect a created need, circumstances that cannot be ignored because they point to other potential conditions. When a product is associated with an event or crisis, those who act on the product do so with a purpose in mind to address both the event and crisis and, perhaps without knowing what they may be, any spinoffs from the event or crisis. There's the fire it must be addressed (someone may be hurt).

A potential for mismanagement of the event occurs if attempts to manage "the event" stop with the products and then this increases the potential for a crisis to emerge. For example, *OUTCOMES result from Products.* The relationship between these two parallels a classic stimulus/response or causal model. "x" occurred and "y" is an outcome. Moreover, since there may be more than one outcome associated with a single product the challenge for those attempting to manage the event or to contain the crisis is to identify and treat as many (and ideally all) of the outcomes associated with the particular phenomenon. It is a challenge, and often a big challenge, so it is useful to involve others, often experts, in the event management or crisis containment efforts.

IMPACTS are the end results associated with the phenomenon's Products and Outcomes. The emerging effects of impacts can be long lasting, and can unfold in unpredictable ways across other areas not originally associated with the products, outcomes or any actions taken in the process. Impacts often are the REAL payoff or costs, either good or bad, associated with the event management or crisis containment efforts. A desired impact is one that benefits the organization in a real way. Attempting to produce a desired impact is the cause, the basis, the motive or rationale for activity, action or efforts taken. Impacts may be tangible (e.g., market share, defeat of an opponent), intangible or abstract (e.g., image enhancement, creation of an emotional state—fear, satisfaction, happiness).[10]

Using Systems Theory to Anticipate a Response Plan

Building a picture of what happened so that planning can occur begins with by mapping the products, outcomes and impacts associated with the event or crisis. Two major courses of action govern the management of an event or crisis containment: decision-making and change. Taking action in these instances means that one is not attempting to dismiss the event or crisis as "not a problem," a "glitch" or simply a nuisance or inconvenience. Denial is not a solution when action is demanded. At the same time, only mapping out the products, outcomes and impacts associated with the emergence of an event or crisis does not equate to making decisions.[11]

In many ways, addressing a troublesome event is the substitution of a negative or unwanted event with a different or changed state. Extinguishing a fire will not take place until several things occur. In our example of a fire in a retirement or skilled nursing community what we are also talking about is a means for moving residents out of harm's way and perhaps evacuated from the building. In addition, contact with professional resources to help with the fire translates into this changed state: they identify the source of the spreading fire, take action and extinguish the fire. Their actions may have nothing to do with evacuating the residents.

Or, at least that is a simplified plan to change an unacceptable situation. Changing a situation from unacceptable to acceptable is more than just managing the event. Changing a situation means addressing the immediate threats, risks and vulnerabilities while, simultaneous, looking to the future and considering the implications of those same threats, risks and vulnerabilities. The decisions made, the information needed to act and the skills and competencies required to implement even a simple plan is different from thinking and acting in ways that protect the organization and its stakeholders in the future. Attempting to manage an event or to contain a crisis requires that those taking action understand the nature of each event or crisis. Thinking in terms of future implications means understanding ramifications for the organization caused by the event and the stakeholder needs. Treating an event as simple, insignificant or without regard for the future is a path for potential unending event mismanagement behavior.

Diagram 4.2 illustrates why the mismanagement of an event can trigger a crisis which, remember, has its own collection of products, outcomes and impacts. The diagram also reminds us a triggered crisis brings us to the edge of a dangerous stream so that a crisis can trigger a catastrophe and, mistreatment of a catastrophe can trigger a disaster.[12] Keep in mind the far right side of the diagram. This is the future for the organization managing the event or attempting to contain a crisis. Lack of early effective management can lead to troublesome times in the future.

The impacts that keep coming may be physical, emotional or psychological for stakeholders. They may be the basis for collective action, for protests, for future litigation. Just dealing with the "now" has to be done with a sense for the natural impacts flowing from the event-stream AND the actions taken by those in the organization and stakeholder network. Look back at Table 4.2 and ask which of these areas are broken, bruised or working and build your plan with these in mind. Those broken or bruised need fixing, and those still in functional condition can be incorporated in the recovery efforts.

What are Needed in Operations and Processes for Stakeholders is a plan of action in the face of a new reality; a reality defined by demands of the event or crisis. Preliminary systemic assessment of the organization in the throes of a troublesome event like a fire or hurricane is likely to reveal erosion of the stakeholders' assessment of the organization's reliability and validity vis a vis needs and the organization's products and services. For example, in the case of a fire or outbreak of a disease, if vendors are denied access to the organization's facilities it can disrupt an entire delivery schedule, with potential rippling effects. When the COVID-19 virus morphed into a pandemic one effect on hospitals was the massive influx of COVID-19 patients, so many in fact that some hospitals had to turn away those in need of elective surgeries and treatment for other health emergencies.[13]

Even when the pandemic ends, or at least becomes contained, what will it take for healthcare systems to regain losses to their image as healthcare providers? When an event threatens or, worse, when a crisis emerges and impacts an organization, the potential for damage to the reliability and validity of the organizational network involved is not limited to the affected organization. For example, the COVID-19 crisis disrupted the relationship between hospitals and skilled nursing and custodial care communities by forcing the latter to seek other solutions for their emergency healthcare needs. When this occurred, all were involved in re-examining the reliability and validity of their local healthcare delivery systems.[14]

Then there are the re-building efforts and costs needed to cover after the event or crisis pass. Certainly, the COVID-19 pandemic is an extreme example, but virtually all threatening events or crises have effects on several aspects of an organization's social network. One negative impact on an organization is damage to the organization's brand or image. What will it take to restore quality and service to meet stakeholder expectations? Will it be safe for our staff to produce or deliver products and services? If systems are broken and inefficient, how long will it take to make them operational? All of these questions reflect a crisis' capacity to impact an organization's brand and image.

It is simple to say that the organization's brand or image is negatively affected and leave it at that, but if the brand is a reference to the organization's reliability and legitimacy as a business partner, then that is a very different issue. If cycle times, from production to delivery are critical to an organization's operations, should stakeholders who rely on that organization question or reassess this business partner who cannot meet their needs because of an event or crisis' effects? During the COVID-19 pandemic, whole industries and businesses suffered because they could not open for business. Then, as if to add insult to injury, even after receiving permission to reopen, prospective patrons stayed away, unsure it would be safe to shop, eat or otherwise use these organizations' facilities. Damage to these organizations lingered because the virus contaminated their image if only by association.

Re-building or restarting an organization after the event or emerging crisis that disrupted service delivery means that promises, assurances or pledges associated with a contract or business agreement are called into question. For example, when COVID-19 impacted medical and skilled nursing and custodial care communities the management and staff of these organizations skipped some procedures or fabricated "workarounds" as a means for providing services. These organizations operate under parameters established by local, state and federal government agencies so were they in violation of regulatory or compliance issues and, if so, how long will it take to be fully compliant in the future?

An often-overlooked cost to an organization engaged in event management or crisis containment are "bureaucratic" costs. Bureaucratic costs are those that occur because reacting to the emergence of the event or crisis meant shifting from work you are paid to do to work that is crisis-related and has to be done. In these instances, management and staff throughout organizations were required to devote time to unscheduled meetings and planning sessions. Then there also is the time spent on managing event or crisis efforts and time lost on the work that one should have been doing but did not because of the event or crisis. And do not forget the unexpected costs associated with bringing on experts or consultants to assist in the efforts.

Finally, there are the re-building costs associated with the event or crisis. These can include costs needed to make computer systems operational on a temporary basis until full systems are available. Rent paid for temporary facilities or vehicles while repairs are made on those damaged is another expense. Sometimes the costs for materials needed to address immediate damages triggered by the event or crisis create a unique waste expense for the organization. These are materials solely bought and then trashed after the event or crisis. Wood needed to protect windows in a hurricane, sandbags used to stem the flow of water, damages to property caused by emergency teams or vehicles, costs to pay for emergency medical staff brought in during evacuations. And, of course, there are the legal fees paid to lawyers or their firms, monies to resolve litigation associated with injured parties that may or may not be part of your organization, or the media cost incurred as your organization attempts to let the public or external stakeholder network know that "things are under control."

Conclusions

The material presented in this chapter meets several objectives. First, tools and information presented illustrate the types of exposures hospitals, nursing homes and self-contained support healthcare operations must address with an emerging troublesome event or crisis. In many instances, reviewing this information is like a checklist for those in organizations looking for a preemptive strategy should they be confronted by these types of phenomena, or a checklist for those confronted with these phenomena and needing to prepare a reactive plan.

Both positions carry their own sense of urgency, demands and costs. Preemptive planning is difficult because the organization's leadership has to motivate staff to engage in work that has no immediate threat. It can be approached as a "just in case" activity, but that line of reasoning goes only so far. The second position, used when the event or crisis is upon the organization, makes it difficult to think of anything other than activities that will deal with the immediate issue at hand.

Two different situations but the material presented can benefit both because at the center of the emergence of a troublesome event or crisis is disruption to the organization and its operations. The disruption may be localized or widespread, but there are disruptions and these have rippling effects on service, relationships, the organization's architecture and operations and, again, its image or brand.

The Agency for Healthcare Research and Quality within the U.S. Department of Health and Human Services is an excellent resource for those wanting more information on ways to plan for or deal with events or crises in either preemptive or reactive ways. What that department's materials and this book do not do is provide material that will make decisions for you. These materials are tools, aids for decision-makers to develop their own plans and solutions.

Decision-makers should always look for ways tools and materials discussed can be used to quantitatively support decisions, actions in general, and real time or post hoc assessments. The Department of Health and Human Services site has several examples to use in conjunction with what is here. Regardless of how the materials here or at HHS are used, all provide one indispensable service to those in leadership and administrative positions: they draw attention to what can be or should be part of all effective organizations.

In that regard, these are not "nice to have" bits and pieces for organizations but, rather, are "musts." The materials in various tables reflect more than a checklist to use in an audit; they are ways to assess where the organization is versus where it needs to be for optimal performance, performance in the face of a troublesome event and how to manage it. So, again, these materials are not designed to tell a manager what to do, they are designed to draw attention to what may be done given one's skills and resources.

Finally, reading this material marks the point in time where you or your organization are now. So, given the material covered, where will your organization be in a year? In three years? If nothing changes in the meantime, you can probably imagine what your organization will look like in the future. If you make some changes you can picture what the organization can look like given those changes but, unfortunately, not how those changes will be reflected in staff attitudes and behavior.

The point here as we leave this chapter consider, given where your organization is now, what changes need to be, could be done and, then, what changes will be done? Among the questions you might ask include any of the following. For example, will your organization have the right people in the right jobs for operational effectiveness? Will staff have the demonstrated competencies needed for their jobs or for the organization and will those competencies be maintained? Are key processes, materials and equipment in place and on the ready? Is the organization's culture vibrant and healthy? Are key health, safety, security, quality and productivity programs in place and regularly audited? Lastly, do staff demonstrate a sense of urgency regarding the organization's mission, their work and stakeholder needs? Are you sure? How do you know?

In the next chapter, we begin to define what actions to take once a crisis morphs from a mismanaged event. The material provided in this and the previous chapter set the stage for that discussion. It is, as you might imagine, an important chapter because its focus is on one central issue: How do we contain a crisis and what does that mean for internal and external stakeholders?

Notes

1. ———. "What_Is_Organizational_Architecture." https://learn.org/articles. 2020.
2. ———. "hr-organization-structure/organizational-design-theory/organizational-architecture-definition." https://hrmhandbook.com/hro.
3. ———. https://www.jaygalbraith.com/images/pdfs/StarModel.pdf.
4. Lowell, Bryan. Enduring Ideas: The 7-S Framework. *McKinsey Quarterly*, March 1, 2008 | Article. https://www.mckinsey.com/business-functions/operations/our-insights/lever-six-organization-and-governance.
5. Trevor, Jonathan and Barry Varcoe. "How Aligned Is Your Organization?" In: Magazine Popular Topics Podcasts Video StoreThe Big Idea Visual Library Case Selections. February 7, 2017.
6. Ibid.

7. Tafoya, Dennis. *Managing Organizational Crisis and Brand Trauma* New York: Palgrave/Macmillan, 2018; Tafoya, Dennis. *Crisis, Catastrophe, and Disaster in Organizations: Managing Threats to Operations, Architecture, Brand and Stakeholders.* New York: Palgrave/Macmillan, 2020.

8. Tafoya, Dennis. "Organizational and Individual Effectiveness, Complexity and the Effects of Emerging Events on Performance." Paper presented the Spring Conference, The Center for the Study of Complex Systems, the Department of Physics, The University of Michigan, May 16, 2009. Tafoya, Dennis. *The Effective Organization.* New York: Routledge, 2010.

9. Tafoya, Dennis. "The Emerging Crisis and the Phenomenon of the Stakeholder Swarm: Tracking the Emergence of Brand Trauma Resulting Fro the Decay of Network Order to Network Chaos." Paper presented at the Annual Swarm Conference, the University of Central Florida, July 6–7, 2013a.

   Tafoya, Dennis. "Retail in the Shadows: Mapping and Describing Sales Transaction Among Those Engaged in the Informal Economy's Drug, Prostitution and Smuggling Trades." Fifth Annual Complexity in Business Conference, University of Maryland, Reagan Conference Center, Washington, DC. November 7–8, 2013b.

   Tafoya, Dennis. *Marginal Organizations: Analyzing Organizations at the Edge of Society.* New York: Palgrave/Macmillan, 2014.

10. Tafoya, Dennis. "Organizational and Individual Effectiveness, Complexity and the Effects of Emerging Events on Performance." Paper presented the Spring Conference, The Center for the Study of Complex Systems, the Department of Physics, The University of Michigan, May 16, 2009. Tafoya, Dennis. *The Effective Organization.* New York: Routledge, 2010.

11. Elbing, Alvar. *Behavioral Decisions in Organizations.* Glenview, Ill: Scott, Foresman and Company, 1978. p. 75.

12. Tafoya, Dennis 2018. *Managing Organizational Crisis and Brand Trauma.* New York: Palgrave/Macmillan, 2018. Tafoya, Dennis. *Crisis, Catastrophe, and Disaster in Organizations: Managing Threats to Operations, Architecture, Brand and Stakeholders.* New York: Palgrave/Macmillan, 2020.

13. Fears, Darryl, Joel Achenbach and Brittney Martin. "As Coronavirus Soars, Hospitals Hope to Avoid an Agonizing Choice: Who Gets Care and Who Goes Home." *The Washington Post*, November 11, 2020 at 9:21 p.m. EST.

   Koop, Chacour. "COVID-19 Patients will be 'sent Home to Die' if Deemed Too Sick, Texas County Says" Fort Worth Star-Telegram JULY 23, 2020 05:28 PM, UPDATED JULY 24, 2020 03:58 PM, https://www.star-telegram.com/news/coronavirus/article244443257.html.

Beasley, Deena. Exclusive: U.S. hospitals turn down remdesivir, limit use to sickest COVID-19 patients. Reuters. SEPTEMBER 11, 20203:55 PMUPDATED 3 MONTHS AGO, https://www.reuters.com/article/us-health-coronavirus-remdesivir-exclusi/exclusive-u-s-hospitals-turn-down-remdesivir-limit-use-to-sickest-covid-19-patients-idUSKBN2622UM.

14. Jain, Amit, Tinglong Dai, Kristin Bibee and Christopher G. Myers. Covid-19 Created an Elective Surgery Backlog. How Can Hospitals Get Back on Track? *Harvard Business Review*. August 10, 2020, https://hbr.org/2020/08/covid-19-created-an-elective-surgery-backlog-how-can-hospitals-get-back-on-track.

Shang, Sarah. "What It Really Means to Cancel Elective Surgeries: To Make Room for coronavirus Patients, Hospitals Are Delaying Procedures That Would Make Major Differences in People's Lives." *The Atlantic*, March 17, 2020, https://www.theatlantic.com/science/archive/2020/03/patients-whose-surgeries-are-canceled-because-coronavirus/608176/.

Berlin, Gretchen and David Bueno, Kyle Gibler, and John Schulz. "Cutting Through the COVID-19 Surgical Backlog." McKinsey and Company. October 2, 2020, https://www.mckinsey.com/industries/health care-systems-and-services/our-insights/cutting-through-the-covid-19-sur gical-backlog.

5

Management and Containment as Problem Solving Change Strategies

Abstract Whether in the near or far term, people change as a result of an event or crisis. Sometimes this change is unavoidable. If someone is injured, the change is obvious. However, some people may want to look past the event or crisis after it is contained or under control and simply revert to an earlier, more convenient way of functioning. There are many ways to approach this chapter's theme, but let's highlight one thing: the tendency to rush to a solution as a means for demonstrating action is not a good idea when faced with a troublesome event or emerging crisis. Managing a troublesome event has its own challenges, but if the event morphs into a crisis, then different effort, thinking, resources and actions are required.

Keywords Change and change strategies · Event management vs crisis containment · Stakeholders and event monitoring · Performance drivers and event management

D. W. Tafoya and L. Poeth, *Healthcare Leadership in Times of Crisis*, https://doi.org/10.1007/978-3-030-75965-0_5

Whether in the near or far term, people change as a result of an event or crisis. Sometimes this change is unavoidable. If someone is injured, the change is obvious. However, some people may want to look past the event or crisis after it is contained or under control and simply revert to an earlier, more familiar way of functioning. There are many ways to approach this chapter's theme, but let's emphasize one thing: the tendency to rush to a solution as a means for demonstrating action is not a good idea when faced with a troublesome event or emerging crisis. Managing a troublesome event has its own challenges, but if the event morphs into a crisis, then different effort, thinking, resources and actions are required.

The approach for addressing a crisis is mapped as a two-part process. The first part defines a containment effort that limits the scope and scale of the crisis. Remember, using our model, cyclones, floods or fires are events that may be unavoidable, but when mismanaged trigger a crisis. The containment protocol outlined here seeks to address the emerging crisis. The second part of the process addresses that period as the crisis' effects spread releasing an array of damaging products. These products, in turn, unfold a mix of outcomes with a potentially staggering number of diverse impacts on the organization, its stakeholders and social networks. This part of the plan outlines ways to address these crisis by-products; it is where the change processes occur. Think of everything involved as managing a turnaround!

Part I: First management, then containment

Planning for Event Management: Understand the Known Events That May Arise

Different features dominate efforts to approach troublesome events that emerge in healthcare institutions. First, the range of events that can arise in these organizations is staggering. Events classified as "healthcare related" can range in intensity or severity, may surface as single events or link to other events or conditions, some not immediately apparent.

Second, our model seeks to prevent a crisis from emerging from these events. This means that events require immediate and effective management. This can be a challenge in healthcare organizations when already busy with regular routine events is overrun with events spawned by mega-events like an airline crash, hurricane or the like. Then, too, there are those other times when a protracted event, like the spread of the coronavirus may overwhelm a healthcare providers' total resources. Regardless of the nature of the event or conditions faced, managing the event is the first step in preventing the triggering of a crisis.

The challenges facing healthcare providers are not limited to specifics associated with a particular medical issue. Healthcare professionals quickly learn that shadowing their actions are a number of special interest groups acting as advocates for the individual needing or receiving care. These are members of a healthcare organization's social network. Some are invited, ongoing members, like regulators, others are experts in particular medical fields or organizations with whom the healthcare organization has an affiliated relationship, as is the case for nursing homes and hospitals.

Other healthcare monitors only join a healthcare organization's network when there is a problem, for example, when an event, say treatment of a medical issue results in complications or additional injury. Litigators are one of the most prominent members to the network in these instances. These lawyers act on behalf of the injured when treatments of medical events are problematic.

It is important to understand the role of this particular group because they illustrate an underlying theme in this discussion of event management and crisis containment for healthcare organizations: risk. Risk in this instance translates as damages and these damages can effect the organization's or its professionals' architecture, operations and brand or image. So, as harbingers of risk there is something to gain in seeing how law firms approach the troublesome events that healthcare organizations and related communities may face. Litigators are knowledgeable adversaries with commitments, much like those in medical professions to build their business, their professional and economic profiles.

In many ways lawyers and law firms with practices devoted to healthcare emergencies are skilled at documenting business risks for healthcare providers. To illustrate their "relationship" to healthcare organizations and their staff consider ways different law firms inform potential clients of types of events that may benefit from legal aid. For example, some law firms look for familiar incidents as issues of concern. Events like slips and falls, bedsores and overdose and medication errors are the three most common nursing home injuries according to the Centers for Disease Control and Prevention in Washington, DC.[1] Other firms present a more extensive list of the most common injuries in nursing homes for potential clients to consider. Their list includes but is not limited to: (1) Bed and Pressure Sores, (2) Sepsis, (3) Restraint Injuries, (4) Malnutrition and Dehydration, (5) Choking, (6) Blocked Breathing Tubes, (7) Burns, (8) Medication Injuries, (9) Falls and (10) Head Injuries.[2] Some of these firms go on to explain that, "negligence in nursing homes often stems from overworked staff, crowded facilities and improper treatment" and "medication errors, not monitoring residents' eating habits, and restraint" have potential to result in the common conditions noted. This additional information helps family members in this instance not only know how or why their loved ones' suffered but why they did not need to suffer if appropriate care was provided. Or, when sending "your loved one for care in a nursing home, you expect staff to attend to his or her needs and keep safety in mind at all times. Yet, injuries are often a significant sign negligence or abuse may be occurring."[3]

Again, these are issues some litigators look for and see as important. Beyond these, it might be prudent for those in management and administrative positions to do their own research to familiarize themselves with the views of others on the topic of healthcare injuries. And, while they are doing this research they also might spend time examining another source of troublesome events associated with healthcare delivery: injuries for nursing and other support staff.

Nancy J. Brent, a nurse with a law degree wrote in an article entitled "Workplace safety is a must for nurses" that "patient safety is vital and cannot be underestimated — and neither can workplace safety for nurses."[4] In 2013, the Bureau of Labor Statistics indicated that specific healthcare settings, such as hospitals and long-term care facilities, had a total case rate of 6.4 work-related injuries and illnesses for every 100 full-time employees. As a result, the Occupational Safety and Health Administration's deputy director issued a memo on June 25, 2016, to guide inspections in healthcare settings. "Brent went on to focus her article on a summary of matters nursing and support staff should address in their workplace. Brent wrote that in addition to "your employer's responsibilities under OSHA, you also have responsibilities to maintain a safe and healthful workplace. The list is long and merits a close read but here are highlights related to material already covered. Among the items on the list are:

- Complying with your employer's policies and procedures based on its obligations under OSHA;
- Using personal protective equipment, including masks, when indicated;
- Carefully administering injections per facility policy;
- Informing your nurse manager and others designated in the facility policy of workplace violence (e.g., bullying, intimidation, verbal abuse);
- Using proper body mechanics when lifting, pushing wheelchairs or otherwise working with patients;
- Reducing risks for slips, trips or falls by removing obstacles, wiping up wet walking surfaces and wearing shoes that support your feet and your walking;
- Speaking with your nurse manager and CNO when policies and procedures governing safety are not being followed."[5]

This list is particularly notable because it is written by someone experienced in both nursing and the law, and because its focus is on *people within a healthcare delivery system's internal social network; its staff.*

Planning for Event Management: Understand Both the Internal and External Stakeholders Involved

For some, this information may not come as a surprise. Someone spending any appreciable amount of time in healthcare organizations is likely to see instances of one or more of these adverse "*events.*" What may not be readily apparent, however, are the scope and scale of stakeholders monitoring these organizations for these types of events and, importantly, their motivations or interest for getting involved. Consider the material in Tables 5.1 and 5.2 as a guide.

Table 5.1 summarizes a list of typical internal stakeholders that may monitor troublesome events affecting residents and staff. These are on

Table 5.1 Representative internal stakeholders potentially monitoring events that threaten residents and staff

The stakeholders monitoring healthcare delivery	Motivations or interests	What is reviewed	Data or information collected
Management	• Reduce incidents • Reduce exposures • Reduce costs • Safe environment • Gain information	• Real-time data	• Incident reports • Health profiles • Health status • Record of the event • Causes of the event • Personnel involved • Staff involved
Medical and support staff	• Patient health and safety • Immediate treatment • Relieve pain & suffering • Operate without injury	• Resources available • Back up support • Communication channels • Family involvement	• Health profile • Medications • Previous incidents • Record of the event • Staff involved
Family Members	• Health & Safety • Justice • Compensation	• Return to health • Legal representation • Reparation for damages • Healthcare assurances	• Health profile • Medications • Previous incidents • Record of the event • Staff involved

(continued)

Table 5.1 (continued)

The stakeholders monitoring healthcare delivery	Motivations or interests	What is reviewed	Data or information collected
Patients Suffering from Injury	• A return to health • Health & Safety • Protection from reprisals	• Return to health • Return to care • Reparation for damages	• Preventative aids
Injured Staff	• Return to health • Prevention in the future	• Possible compensation • Legal representation • Union representation	• Profile of incidents • Any training
Litigators (Internal)	• Documented incidents • Incident history • Incident profiles • Prior litigation • Management Actions	• Access to injured • Access to family • Access to staff • Documentation	• Record of the event • Staff involved • Staff profiles • Incidents by types • Prior warnings • Training programs • Orientation efforts • Safety programs • Security programs

the front line of troublesome events that arise in healthcare organizations. There is a range of professionals as part of this internal network and that is important to keep in mind because their collective perspectives provide insight into almost every aspect of a healthcare facility. When reviewing a collection of stakeholders like those represented in the table note the levels of involvement they may have with each other or the organization. The litigators in the table tend to be "incident-specific" members while the medical and support staff are involved over the long term. Next,

Table 5.2 Representative external stakeholders potentially monitoring events that threaten patients and staff

The stakeholder monitoring healthcare delivery	Motivations or interests	What is reviewed	Data or information collected
Regulators	• Adherence to rules • Proactive plans • Preemptive plans	• Organization's History • Training programs • Orientation efforts • Safety programs • Security programs	• Incidents by types • Prior warnings
Litigators (External)	• Documented incidents • Incident history • Incident profiles • Prior litigation • Management Actions	• Access to injured • Access to family • Access to staff • Documentation • Compensation	• Documentation • Prior Claims • Case histories • Behavioral profiles
Insurance Providers	• Protection of its assets • Responsible management • Reduction in reportables • "Hot Spots" • Overall Risk Exposure	• Incidents by types • Prior warnings • Training programs • Orientation efforts • Safety programs • Security programs	• Documentation • Prior Claims • Case histories • Behavioral profiles • Comparable data

The stakeholder monitoring healthcare delivery	Motivations or interests	What is reviewed	Data or information collected
Labor Unions	• Protect members • Add members • Seek entry to organization • Revenue	• Incidents by types • Prior warnings • Training programs • Orientation efforts • Safety programs • Security programs	• Record of the event • Staff involved • Staff profiles • Incidents by types • Prior warnings • Training programs • Orientation efforts • Safety programs • Security programs
Social agencies and groups, Media and other special interests	• Health of populations • "Community well-being" • Protection of "vulnerables" • A story for the public	• "To be a voice" • Industry standards • Industry guidelines • Legislative action • Public action • Involvement of others • A story • Appeal for readership	• Media coverage • Interested parties • National data • Documentation • Prior Claims • Case histories • Behavioral profiles • Comparable data
Hospital and Medical, EMT personnel	• Patient health and safety • Immediate treatment • Relieve pain & suffering • Provide support to staff	• Immediate resources • Back up support • Communication channels • Ensure family is called	• Health profile • edications • Previous incidents • Record of the event • Staff involved

consider which are likely to be involved should a crisis emerge and their roles in the crisis process.

Table 5.2 summarizes a list of external stakeholders that may monitor threatening events associated with healthcare delivery systems. Some of these stakeholders are involved immediately. For example, if a death occurs or there is a breakout of an infectious disease. Others, like litigators, insurance providers or the media join into an event management effort over time or as needed. Note, too, that many of these stakeholders enter into a relationship with the healthcare organization as adversaries. And keep in mind that it probably is not wise to over weight the salience of particular stakeholders based on their titles, education or other surface features. Remember, a lawyer may be representing one client but a union officer represents all union members. Both carry significant weight when the organization's future is in balance.

Planning for Event Management: Sketching the Plan and Defining Roles and Responsibilities

The path outlined to this point, tracing the relationship between events and stakeholders, makes sense because that is typically an important flow worth monitoring when an event occurs. The next steps in this process reflect those points where action takes place or, where an action plan is sketched and those involved in the plan are identified.

The purpose for this action plan is straightforward: Do something in a responsible manner. The guide for building the plan can include the following:

First, identify the basic nature of the event. What happened/is happening? Who is involved? Where did the event occur? Why did it occur? If there are injuries, address the injuries and then search out the details. For example, in events like a slip and fall, some of this information is collected immediately and easily. If the injury is classified as a "medical oversight" get some real sense regarding what that concept means. Remember, every stakeholder involved is involved in a race for valid and reliable information so do what you can to win that race or, at a minimum, to be at least a front-runner. If someone is injured or unconscious, you may not be able to get complete information, but, regardless, document the entire process and all people involved. Be prepared to document what was done/not done, why and the rationale. Be sure to involve all key professionals you might have available. Lawyers and members from Human Resources to department managers should be at the top of your contact list. Be sure to get signoffs where necessary. Oh, and it might make sense in some instances to run basic issues and details by your professional representatives early in the process so you know the information you can and cannot gather and how to handle what you do collect.

Second, search for the real and related problems. Often the first view of an event may reveal symptoms or manifestations of some underlying issues. A fall is an event. The reason for the fall is as important in an event management process. Both need to be addressed, but not at the expense of any significant issues which may not be immediately evident. Broken bones, hemorrhaging, secondary strains are examples of other issues to address. By the way, not successfully addressing these secondary issues creates trigger points for the makings of a crisis.

Third, determine stakeholders to involve and why. This is a key step for two reasons. Every organization has sets of internal and external stakeholders as outlined in Tables 5.1 and 5.2. It is important to know which of these stakeholders are, should be or, may be involved because of their relationship to the event or their knowledge and experience. Information in Table 5.3 is prepared as another guide in this instance. Your objective is always to try to identify primary and secondary stakeholders from both the internal and external social networks. Some of these stakeholders may support your organization's effort while others are adversaries. It may not be necessary to establish or maintain contact with all individuals, but including them in a communication plan can be useful. Get an idea for any timelines at this point. Note key points in the timeline, from start to finish if possible. Are any permissions or reviews necessary, for example from medical or legal staff, executive management or family members? Now the bottom line: see if you can establish each stakeholder's primary

Table 5.3 Planning for event management: People, areas and responsibilities

People, areas and their role in the planning process	Representative Skills, Tasks or Areas of Responsiblity
People—Administration	• Experienced administrators with healthcare backgrounds • Skilled in managing timely problem or issue management • Hands on professionals able to handle personnel matters *In Planning: They're involved throughout the process*
People—Staffing	• Provide clear instructions • Skilled with appropriate training and certifications • Targeted performance levels that "meet" or "exceed" expectations • Stable work environments with reduced or managed turnover • Exceptional performance during emergencies *In Planning: They're involved in appropriate areas*
People—Patients, Family and Friends	• Follow instructions • Receiving prescribed care • Receiving prescribed medication • Living in a safe environment to avoid accidents or injury • Having personal and social needs met *In Planning: They're involved as knowledge sources*
Processes: How they work	• Safety programs in place and evaluated • Quality programs in place and evaluated • Security programs in place and evaluated • Customer service programs in place and evaluated • Operational practices in place and evaluated *In Planning: Examined for their contribution to the problem or fix*
Material needs	• Needed materials in place and evaluated • Materials for special needs in place and evaluated • Inventory processes in place for goods and materials *In Planning: Examined for their contribution to the problem or fix*
Equipment & Facility needs	• Appropriate equipment in place • Regular maintenance programs in place for key equipment • Operators trained and certified for key equipment *In Planning: Examined for their contribution to the problem or fix*

(continued)

Table 5.3 (continued)

People, areas and their role in the planning process	Representative Skills, Tasks or Areas of Responsiblity
Finance and Budgets	• Annual budgets in place • Budgeted lines for operations improvements • Budgeted lines for emergencies or unexpected needs *In Planning: Examined for their contribution to the problem or fix*
Rules & Regulations	• Rules and regulations are defined and followed • Part of new hire training and orientation • Timely management of infractions • Regular review of rules and regulations *In Planning: Examined for their contribution to the problem or fix*
Organizational Culture	• Supportive organizational culture • Culture supports communication and collaboration • Culture supports fairness and objectivity • A safe, hostility-free environment *In Planning: Examined for its contribution to the problem or fix*

needs regarding the event. This can be an invaluable piece of information for you to collect.

Fourth, identify what needs immediate attention. Action plans like those we are reviewing focus on change. Change may mean stopping the pain, other times it means at best stabilizing a condition. This is the point where the event management occurs to prevent triggering a crisis. It may not mean that everything associated with the event is under control, only that a crisis is averted. Finally, the reason this is the fourth step on this list does not imply that this is some type of sequential process. It appears here to demonstrate the need for information when an event occurs. Medical attention is provided when needed and the rationale for aid is understood and justified.

Results of Event Management: Gauging the success of your Performance Drivers

Ideally, what we want to see when an event has been successfully managed is that threats, conditions, ramifications or whatever else negative or potentially harmful features associated with the event are addressed. But as we've seen, events are complicated. Wounds from an accident have to be treated and maintained, patient health after a stroke has to be monitored and maintained, and someone has to clean up after the fire has been extinguished and the damages repaired. So how can we assess successful event management? That is, the event was managed in a way so that a crisis was not triggered?

Using an approach we call "process criteria assessment" a benchmark is prepared for all in the organization to use when engaged in event management efforts. This approach builds off established knowledge of the organization's important Processes, Products and Services. The criteria are standards or principles applied to all areas of the organization involved in the management effort (e.g., the people, processes, materials, equipment, etc.) as illustrated in Table 5.3.

A typical assessment may cover many topics. For example, what can be said of performance vis a vis the equipment used. Did equipment perform as needed? Were sufficient equipment and supplies available? What about processes and procedures? What response processes worked, and which did not? How was staff involved in the management effort? What required skills were demonstrated and which should be improved? What competencies were demonstrated, which need improvement and what others are needed? If patients or staff were the focus of the event what is their status? If there were injuries who was injured and what is their status? Finally, in all instances, a status or summary report is prepared and submitted to all appropriate stakeholders—within and outside of the organization.

Once the criteria are defined in terms of the event and its features (e.g., people involved, type of event, risks, etc.) applying process and product criteria to complete the assessment is a straightforward task. This means that every event is assessed in terms of its type and particular characteristics. To do these assessments, focus on different stages of "recovery status" for each type of event. For example consider these seven "event states" discussed below and note how they differ from each other given this event as well as the relationship that may exist among some.

Routine events: These are known or familiar events to those in the organization. Slip and falls, minor burns or muscle strains are examples. In some instances, outside assistance may be required to complete the event management process, for example if transportation was required or any final evaluations are necessary to document satisfactory event management.

Intense events: In these events circumstances associated with the event may require outside assistance for the event's management process, or for assistance with people involved. In addition, special circumstances, for example associated with medical treatment processes and/or for assistance in transporting individuals or providing secondary and/or final evaluations may be required. In some instances, law enforcement or other areas may provide support or assistance. Immediate staff may provide preliminary assistance to someone suffering from a major heart attack but it may be prudent to move the patient to an area with a full range of diagnostic equipment and staff with advanced skills and competencies.

Extreme events: These often require outside assistance. The nature of the event and the risks associated with it require skilled, outside assistance or interventions. These are frequently potentially life-threatening events or events which may become life-threatening (e.g., severe infections, threats of gun violence or fires). This is particularly true if emergency teams in fire and law enforcement are required support with the immediate event or follow-up.

Recovery event status also can be approached as events and then in terms of products, outcome and impact criteria. In these instances, the status of the recovery process, the extent to which the recovery is successful or contained and evident risks remaining with individuals, facilities, materials or equipment associated with the event are noted. There are three levels of recovery examined: complete, partial and no recovery.

Complete Recovery event status: Products, outcomes and impact of the event are identified and addressed. Complete functioning and recovery for the affected person(s), area, etc., has occurred. This also implies that the individual(s) or facilities involved have been assessed and certified as recovered by appropriate individuals. Now it is important to note that even with the claim of "complete recovery" that may not mean there are no secondary issues remaining for the injured party. Pain and suffering, different levels and types of trauma also may be factors. Finally, this last observation is another reason why taking a product, outcomes and impacts assessment is valuable. If the recovery speaks to the "products" associated with the event, for example, a broken leg, that does not mean that "outcomes" and "impacts" are part of the recovery claim.

Partial Recovery event status: Most products, outcomes and impact of the event are identified and/or addressed. In addition to written summaries by those involved, quantitative assessments are included in any final report. For example, functioning and recovery for the effected person(s), area, etc., may be described as "approximately xx% as determined by xx authorities," where the authorities and their qualifications are noted. Finally, if possible, some estimate of the time to full recovery is made. For example, "Full recovery is expected within xx days as certified by xx individual(s)." In reference to the comments made regarding a "Complete Recovery" those doing the assessments also should keep in mind that "products, outcomes and impacts" also are defined in the eyes of the beholder. In other words, just because you say "these are the products, outcomes and impacts associated with the event" that does not mean an adversary would agree and, in fact, may have his/her own definitions of each given the event.

No Recovery: The event is not stable and potential for a crisis seems inevitable. In these instances the products, outcomes and impacts associated with the event typically trigger an array of secondary effects. Even death, often approached as an end event, may morph into a crisis. Investigations, allegations and requests for more information can encumber an organization's staff at all levels. "No recovery" assessments also can trigger unanticipated emotional and psychological affects for stakeholders whether in or outside of the organization. Detailed reports in these instances are important. With "no recovery" status, a mix of outside stakeholders can be involved. These can represent such diverse areas as regulatory agencies (e.g., law enforcement, fire, federal agencies), health and medical agencies (e.g., state and local health departments) and private interests (e.g., lawyers, family doctors for secondary opinions, elder agencies).

Conclusion: Searching for Solutions to Events and Incidents

As we saw in Chapter 3, there are a lot of reasons why a mismanaged event or a crisis, catastrophe or disaster materializes. In this chapter, we explored useful ways to explain how and why these things happen and ways to devise management or containment strategies and tactics for these phenomena. Frequently, and for many different reasons, many in organizations seem to believe that doing something by rushing to a solution is an effective way for demonstrating action or at least an interest in doing the right thing. We do not believe it is for several reasons.

If an event occurs and is managed it is easy to let the occurrence fade from view and to just get on with pressing day-to-day matters. For example, quickly picking up a patient who has fallen may seem like a good solution, but without knowing how or why the individual fell or if there are hidden injuries may make a seemingly routine situation worse. This seems obvious, but what about those instances when there is a more serious challenge facing the organization's staff, like a fire in the building or a terrorist with a loaded weapon? Any first tendency is to rush and to try and put the fire out or to deal with the intruder ripples with well-meaning intentions, but fires are what fire departments are for—a health center's staff are better skilled in evacuating people from harm's way. That is their role when a fire or other serious threat surfaces.

Some solutions add little value at the time. For example, suppose someone is dropping off a patient and pulls into a "no parking" area. In these instances, ask at least two questions: Should anything be done or can the problem wait? A staff member may not demonstrate the best judgment if he or she puts off a full slate of tasks to run down someone who may be creating only momentary traffic issue.

On the other hand, maybe getting the person to move their car is not the real problem to address. Is the area clearly marked "no parking?" Are all instances when someone parks in that area addressed? In other words, should people driving into the parking lot believe the sign, or might they think it applies in special instances, like an emergency. Also, are there other areas where patient loading and unloading is possible and, if so, are these areas (a) clearly marked and (b) made known to those likely to be dropping patients off at the facility?

Sometimes a solution that seems like a good idea is beyond the organization's immediate means to implement. Improving building or computer system security are critical matters but they are matters best left up to professionals skilled in those areas. Keep in mind, too, that attempting to address some issues without having the right skills and competencies can result in added risk exposures. If the organization takes it upon itself to build its security program and security is breached, they developed the system so they own the event and fallout.

Is a proposed solution to a problem the only solution or could there be more? Sometimes it pays (in many ways) to invite others to offer their ideas or solutions for a problem, particularly if they are experienced or experts in related fields. Take the parking issue mentioned above. Talking to members in the township offices or the police for their ideas not only may result in good solutions but there may be additional benefits. By seeking their thoughts, you may be demonstrating your interest in doing the right thing and, at the same time, enhancing your relationship with them, and that can have very long-term benefits.

Lastly, if there are many solutions offered to address an issue, how will you determine which is best? When seeking a solution, and particularly when you are opening up your search to others, it helps if you define a strong (and meaningful) list of criteria to use in evaluating a solution. Budget issues are one criterion, as are any skills or expertise needed to design and implement the solution. Remember, if you use an existing staff member to help solve a problem then (a) that staff member may be taken off an existing assignment that may still have to be covered and (b) ancillary issues like solution costs, roles and responsibilities and the amount of time required implement or manage the solution may need to be established before hand. Remember, the person leading the problem-solving team is the team leader but not the one with the final say on the matter. People must know and understand their limits in projects associated with troublesome events and crises.

Proactive, Pre-event Preparation in Healthcare Delivery Systems

Apart from coming up with solutions to events or incidents that emerge, a truly proactive approach to take first is Pre-Event Preparation and Planning. We know it is not possible to predict all the events that may arise to threaten an organization so other options are warranted. Pre-Event Preparation and Planning is a prudent safeguard to launch for large classes of potential events (e.g., fires) or for those which appear to regularly occur (e.g., slips and falls).

Table 5.5 in Appendix provides a sketch of plans and activities that could be part of a health organization's operational efforts when building a "pre-event preparation plan." At a minimum the material is a useful checklist or, in some instances, as an evaluation tool to assess potential strengths, weaknesses and vulnerabilities in the organization and/or among its personnel or departments.

The types of plans outlined in the appendix are representative of ways events may be managed, or crises contained. Overall, these plans illustrate a dynamic change effort. The operations management effort involves those routine and extraordinary efforts enacted in order to meet pre-defined or expected organizational needs. In short, the plans reflect types of activities that keep the doors open to meet client needs and to manage the overall stakeholder network should a crisis emerge. Finally, the pre-event preparation and planning reflects efforts:

a. to immediately address the threats that emerge,
b. to focus on crisis containment preventing it from morphing into a potentially more dangerous catastrophe or, worse, a disaster,
c. to design and build a response which enables the organization and its stakeholders to function while managing risk exposures, limiting damages, addressing physical, emotional or cognitive damages,

d. to address traumatic damages and impact to the organization's (and/or its stakeholders') architectural, operational or brand/image, and

e. to gain knowledge through a type of simulation of possible approaches that may be taken in troublesome or worst case scenarios.

In summary, the objective throughout is to gain and maintain the initiative over whatever is the organization's current state of exposures or operational conditions. This last point can be especially valuable for those in healthcare or any organizations to consider and to think of where they are now and where they might be should a crisis emerge that needs to be contained. Those in healthcare industries are familiar with the use of scenarios, beta tests and experiments as tools to safely study a drug or process in a lab before it is introduced into a public area. That also is part of the value of pre-event preparation and planning. Do the planning in a safe, crisis-free environment and then, if it works, roll it out when it is needed.

Finally, pre-event preparation and planning provides one especially powerful benefit to an organization's leadership and staff—the opportunity to conduct periodic reviews of potential risks, threats and vulnerabilities associated with the organization's operations or environment. For example, Table 5.4 illustrates the type of "environment scan" that might be developed to keep an organization's leadership or key stakeholders informed regarding the organizations overall health and status.[6] This type of material can flow directly out of the preparation or review of plans outlined in Table 5.5 in Appendix.

In the end, information collected from both activities, the scan and plan, are useful for preventative and reactive response efforts. The material is preventative to the extent that should an event or crisis emerge, at least those in the organization may be better prepared for what to expect. The material outlined in the appendix is a potent reactive response tool in that the plans reflect who can or should be involved, with their roles and responsibilities defined. The organization that prepares such plans may be better prepared if events or crises emerge. Material in the next chapter takes this information to its maximum benefit: containment of a crisis, catastrophe or disaster.

Table 5.4 A sample environmental scan: Gauging precursors to a crisis

The organizational status or conditions	The environment's status	Responses to observed conditions
Normal, things are OK	Healthy environment Business as usual *Crisis conclusion: None*	• Maintain the Status Quo • Practice Continuous Process Improvement • Conduct periodic audits. (Data are rolled up to top management)
Tension, anxiety, strain, pressure	Discussions, complaints, suggestions are noted. Look for symptoms. (Arguments, missed due dates, staff shortages) *Crisis conclusion: Crisis possible*	• Data collection around tension points • Prepare status updates • Identify "hot spots," trigger points or thresholds leading to a crisis • Data rolled up to top management • Launch containment efforts
Stress, hassles, difficulty, trauma	Tensions escalate in multiple ways. List breached thresholds. *Crisis conclusion: Crisis likely*	• Data collection throughout operations • Seek outside professional help • Alert and keep stakeholders informed (e.g., attorneys, human resources) • Target key containment objectives
Critical, significant, vital, dangerous	Reported incidents. Summarize damages *Crisis conclusion: Crisis probable*	• Implement Emergency Controls • Involve all affected stakeholders • Report on containment efforts
Calamity	Multiple incidents *Crisis Conclusion: Crisis evident*	• Implement crisis management plan • Identify secure and non-secure areas • Lock in containment efforts

Table 5.5 Pre-event preparation and planning

Pre-Incident Planning (Site and Building Information for First Responders)

The issue: Does your organization have an accessible plan outlining site and building information for first responders? At a minimum this plan should:

1. Identify immediately apparent system risks, threats and vulnerabilities
2. Identify key personnel in the organization and their roles and capabilities
3. Traffic plans and maps should be available and, ideally, communicated to first responders for their files
4. Building maps should describe entry and exit points and "hot" spots in the building(s) (e.g., places where hazardous materials may be stored or used)
5. A distribution list of all external organizations receiving a copy of this pre-planning should be included
6. The plan should be reviewed annually and updated as needed. Updated plans are released to those on the distribution list, outdated plans should be retrieved and destroyed. Planning also should account for the movement of guests and visitors

Protective Planning for Life Safety Incidents

The issue: Staff and residents should be trained in evacuation plans. This includes:

1. Knowledge of evacuation routes and procedures
2. Stipulation of how staff and residents should respond in the event of a life safety incident
3. Lists and locations of emergency equipment useful in life safety incidents
4. Lists and locations of external shelters or safe rooms
5. Orientation of new staff members, and training for all staff in planning for life safety incidents

Medical Planning and Actions

The issue: Designative staff must be trained and certified in current American Heart Association (AHA) Guidelines for Cardiopulmonary Resuscitation (CPR) and Emergency Cardiovascular Care (ECC). This training and certification includes the use of external defibrillators, containment of pathogens viruses, bacteria, fungi and parasites. Additionally, of particular focus are pathogens that include, but are not limited to, hepatitis B (HBV), hepatitis C (HCV) and human immunodeficiency virus (HIV). Needle sticks and other sharps-related injuries may expose workers to blood-borne pathogens

(continued)

Table 5.5 (continued)

Firefighting Plans and Activities

The issue: Define the types of fires within your staff's capacity to manage, and when outside resources must be involved. Always be prepared to evaluate areas where the fire is and/or the entire facility. Rely on the "pre-incident planning" defined about how to prepare for the involvement of needed external resources. Planning also should account for the movement of guests and visitors. Important: As noted, for extreme events like fire management of these events is the responsibility of skilled professionals, not the organization's staff. The organization's primary interest is protection of patients and guests by removing them from dangerous areas

Hazardous Materials Plan

The issue: A plan which lists all hazardous and dangerous (e.g., pharmaceuticals) must be prepared and made available to all external resources (e.g., fire and police). In addition, the location of all safety materials should be defined with responsibility for these materials designated. MSDS should be updated annually or as needed. Local agencies (e.g., fire and law enforcement) should be immediately notified when these hazards are realized

Natural Hazards Planning

The issue: Natural hazard plans that reflect the needs of different regions of the country and/or the location of buildings and property should be prepared. Plans that prepare for hurricanes, tornadoes, the impact of ice and snowstorms should be prepared. These plans should cover training, communication and evacuation activities as well as preparations for flooding, loss of power and damages associated with wind events. Moreover, if shelter in place is the option, equipment and materials (e.g., medications and first aid) should be available

Planning for Workplace Violence and Threats

The Issue: The organization's staff should be trained to respond to workplace violence from patients, staff and outside individuals. Again, this is a two-part process: notify appropriate emergency agencies and remove patients and guests from exposure to these threats. Work with local police, medical and psychological professionals to develop the training and plans needed. This planning also should contain training to deal with bomb threats, suspicious packages and harassment of any form

Planning for Common Human-caused events: Mold, Odors and Spills

The Issue: It is important that in addition to providing a secure environment for residents and staff, most nursing homes and eldercare communities also are public centers for guests, visitors and affiliated external visitors (e.g., medical personnel, regulatory representative, police and fire.) Mold, odors and spills are representative of routine human-caused events in nursing and eldercare communities that must be addressed immediately for the protection of residents, staff and visitors. Moreover, it is important to remember that these types of events can communicate a negative impression regarding the ways in which the organization handles housekeeping, maintenance, the general safeguarding of patients and personnel on a daily basis

(continued)

Table 5.5 (continued)

Planning for Acts of Personal Harm

The Issue: Incident response plans and training to avert and deal with incidents of racism, sexism, discrimination of any form must be prepared. These and related acts must be immediately documented and addressed. In addition, hostile acts of any kind (for example, robbery or theft, extortion, hostage incidents, workplace violence, and elder abuse of any form) must be documented and addressed with victims protected from future acts. In all cases, local and, if necessary, state and federal agencies should be involved as resources

Planning for Technology-Related Events

The Issue: Incident response plans to address unintentional disruptions in telecommunications, electrical power, water, pollution control system, sewerage system, other critical infrastructure must be prepared. In addition to incident response activities, these plans should be part of overall efforts to protect and maintain these systems. Moreover, threats to cyber security (data corruption/theft, loss of electronic data interchange or e-commerce, loss of domain name server, spyware/malware, vulnerability, hacking and denial of service) must be prepared. It also is important to note that plans associated with cyber security must reflect the need to protect and prevent incidents for residents as well as the organization

Preparation of a Pre-Event Plan of Action

The Issue: Given the range of events that may arise in our organization the materials reviewed provide guidance for the following areas should a troublesome event or crisis emerge. Now, match the above with our core organizational features to build your overall plan:

People:

Processes:

Material:

Equipment:

Programs:

Safety

Security

Quality

Productivity

Processes:

Communication

Knowledge Mgmt

Information Mgmt

Evaluation

Pre-event Preparation and Planning: An Example of Successful Management in the face of Changing Circumstances

Introduction: There is a tendency to focus planning and incident response efforts on matters frequently encountered in healthcare product and service delivery efforts. This is natural, but in today's world, no organization is immune and protected from threats stemming from exceptional natural events or human error. The potential range of threats, hazards and menaces facing the staff, residents and guests associated with these organizations is extensive.

A recent discussion with a professional at one university health center illustrates this point. The emergence of the COVID-19 virus put many in healthcare on guard for the virus' potential impact so, all things considered, every attempt was made to prevent faults in the capacity to meet stakeholder needs whenever possible. For example, as soon as the virus emerged as a pandemic this professional devised a unique staffing plan to anticipate the possible impact of the virus on the department's capacity to meet stakeholder needs in a timely fashion. To do this, the department's staff was divided into two groups, labeled "Red" and "Blue." Using this plan, if someone in one group became exposed or infected with the virus everyone in the group could be tested and, if necessary, steps could be taken to track the overall integrity of the group's health. At the same time, the second group could be mobilized to so that production and service would be uninterrupted.

The plan worked well into the pandemic but what no one saw coming were random, secondary effects the virus might have on operations. One such effect was the virus' impact on on-time delivery of goods ordered during the Christmas, Hanukkah and Kwanzaa holiday shopping season. In this instance, the "stay-at-home" requirements different local and state governments imposed on their communities to reduce the spread of the virus meant that citizens could not shop in stores but were expected to do virtually all shopping online.

Now, the influx of shopping online coupled with the convergence of the holiday season and the inability for shoppers to go to a store to pick up their purchases translated into a dilemma for all involved. Online shopping was so intense that the shipping industry became backlogged with purchases, which also influenced the delivery of goods for business and industry.[7]

Chris Isidore writing for CNN Business summarized the barrier facing consumers when he wrote "Good luck getting your holiday gifts delivered on time this year. You'll need it. A surge in online purchases during the pandemic means that parcel delivery services are struggling to keep up with shipments. Demand for shipping has reached levels they didn't expect to deliver until several years from now. Now everyone in the industry – senders, recipients and those who deliver the shipments – are growing concerned about an even bigger surge in shipments as the holiday season gets underway."[8]

The university mentioned above dodged this unexpected threat to their supply chain by turning to the standing supplier for the goods they needed. In this instance the suppliers did not miss a beat through the COVID-19 December 2020 holiday rush, but threats to the supply chain still proved to be an unexpected matter for them and others to keep in mind if they hoped to receive goods likely to be shipped via commercial carriers. Overall, this and similar experiences illustrate that no planning or preparations are ever one hundred percent perfect. It is impossible to have contingency plans for all events but what works overall is operating an organization on tested fundamental practices and procedures and always remaining vigilant for changes and challenges to occur.

Appendix 1: Pre-Event Preparation and Planning

Introduction The material in this appendix is an example of ways many plans can be used to develop a single, organization-wide pre-event plan. In this appendix different types of plans are sketched which, when taken as part of a whole, may prove relevant for effective healthcare delivery when faced with a troublesome event or emerging crisis. The process begins with assessments of evident vulnerabilities or exposures. These initial assessments guide subsequent actions and the development of the overall plan.

Notes

1. Koonz, Mckenny Johnson and Depaolis. "3 Most Common Nursing Home Injuries" Posted on September 8, 2017, https://koonz.com/3-common-nursing-home-injuries/.
2. Trantolo and Trantolo. "10 of the Most Common Injuries in Nursing Homes." https://www.trantololaw.com/law-firm-blog/nursing-home-negligence/10-common-injuries-in-nursing-homes/.
3. Ibid.
4. Brent, Nancy J. Nurse.com "Workplace Safety a Must for Nurses." Nurse.com. November 16, 2016, https://www.nurse.com/blog/2016/11/16/what-nurses-need-to-know-about-workplace-safety/.
5. Ibid.
6. Tafoya, Dennis. *Organizations in the Face of Crisis: Managing the Brand and Stakeholders*. New York: Palgrave/Macmillan, 2013.
7. Finney, Michael and Randall Yip. "Consumers Worry About Holiday Delivery Delays as Shopping Moves Online Amid Pandemic." *ABC Television News*, "7 ON YOUR SIDE" Tuesday, October 27, 2020, https://abc7news.com/holiday-shopping-covid-19-delivery-delays-online/7365574/.

   Garland, Max. "FedEx Ground contractors say COVID-19 Is Causing A Volume Spike Surpassing the Holidays." Memphis Commercial Appeal, May 21, 2020, https://www.commercialappeal.com/story/money/industries/logistics/2020/05/21/fedex-ground-shipping-demand-online-shopping-deliveries/5224789002/.

   Isidore, Chris. "Want Something Delivered by Christmas? Order Way in Aadvance." *CNN Business*, Updated 10:33 AM ET, Tuesday October 27, 2020, https://www.cnn.com/2020/10/25/business/holiday-package-delivery-crunch-fedex-ups-post-office/index.html.

   Mia Weinand, Mia. "COVID-19 Disrupts Holiday 2020 Supply Chain Planninghow Retailers Are Prepping To Meet Seasonal Demand," September 22, 2020, https://nrf.com/blog/covid-19-disrupts-holiday-2020-supply-chain-planningRetailGetsReal.

8. Isidore, Chris. "Want Something Delivered by Christmas? Order way in advance," CNN Business, Updated 10:33 AM ET, Tuesday October 27, 2020, https://www.cnn.com/2020/10/25/business/holiday-package-delivery-crunch-fedex-ups-post-office/index.html.

6

Challenges at the Top: Performance Standards for Executives, Boards and Advisors

Abstract Two themes define this chapter. First, managing the challenges associated with a troublesome event, crisis, catastrophe or disaster is more than making decisions or building plans in response to threats or fear of loss. The second is that ownership for the event management or crisis containment efforts rests with the organization's executives. In the face of a troublesome event or emerging crisis people often ask, "Who 'owns' the event management or crisis containment effort" or "Where does the "buck stop"? Our answer to both questions is that ownership for these efforts rests with the organization's executives and, importantly, also with the organization's Boards and advisors. What we expect to see at the top of today's healthcare organizations is "change leadership."

Keywords Change management · Change management · Containment challenges · Containment process · Containment and organizational leadership · Preparing an action plan · Leadership and communication

© The Author(s), under exclusive license to Springer Nature Switzerland AG 2021
D. W. Tafoya and L. Poeth, *Healthcare Leadership in Times of Crisis*,
https://doi.org/10.1007/978-3-030-75965-0_6

Two themes define this chapter. First, managing the challenges associated with a troublesome event, crisis, catastrophe or disaster is more than making decisions or building plans in response to threats or fear of loss. We view effective event management or crisis containment efforts as exercises in "change management." Effective treatment of events or crises that emerge require an orientation aimed at changing a bad or worrisome state to a healthy and maintained state. It is an orientation that recognizes that the disruptions associated with events or crisis must not only end, but that the organization affected by these phenomena must change to a healthy, progressive state.

The second is that ownership for the event management or crisis containment efforts rests with the organization's executives. In the face of a troublesome event or emerging crisis people often ask, "Who 'owns' the event management or crisis containment effort" or "Where does the "buck stop"? Our answer to both questions is that ownership for these efforts rests with the organization's executives and, importantly, also with the organization's Boards and advisors. What we expect to see at the top of today's healthcare organizations is "change leadership." Leadership that embraces change, innovation and discovery as strategies for the foundation for action. This is leadership that enables people so they have the support needed to act, provides them with needed authorization to act and, also ensures they have opportunities to develop the skills and competencies to act.

The Containment Objective

Crisis containment is all about four things: A Crisis, a Plan, Leadership and Change. Throughout this book, a simple linear relationship defines the link between an event or incident and a crisis. If the organization's leadership or staff dodges the event or mismanages it, a crisis will emerge. If the leadership or staff lies or misrepresents what occurred or its seriousness, the event may be mismanaged, and a crisis can emerge. If the organization's leadership or staff fails in the crisis containment effort, the containment may fail and, all things considered, a catastrophe, or worse, a disaster can emerge. The containment process is straightforward and based on a simple assumption: crises do not "just happen."

Successful crisis containment is dependent on a plan. These plans are rapidly constructed, methodical responses to contain, diminish and learn from the crisis. The appendix in Chapter 5 outlines a number of categories for which plans can be/should be developed to avoid or respond to a crisis. Containment is important is for several reasons. First, a crisis can cause damage to the organization's architecture, operations and brand. Second, crises create collateral damage through spin-off incidents and events. A fire causes immediate burn damage, then there is the possibility for injuries because of inhalation of smoke or toxins, and there is always the possibility for deaths to occur. Finally, if a crisis containment effort mismanaged, it can morph into a catastrophe and that into a disaster, both with their own direct and collateral damages.

While everything may look the same in your organization, when a crisis grips operations, the organization is different. Think about a crisis you have observed and perhaps one in your own organization. What were normal procedures and processes that changed? Time devoted to crisis-related tasks of planning, problem-solving, firefighting, decision-making is added to ongoing routine tasks and activities. In addition, many things that are not what people expect to do as part of their jobs like becoming a member of a special project team or attending information meetings. To them these types of tasks on add layers of work to jobs they are already expected to do. In short, when a crisis emerges, those in the organization must do things differently; they must shift into a turnaround mentality. The organization in a crisis is not the same as the organization before the crisis. This may seem like a trite, obvious observation but built into it is the fact that when responding to a crisis few actually take note of the costs crisis containment may have on budget expenditures, productivity, work throughput and other key operational variables. Engaged management is critical to lead a successful turnaround; management oversees activities but drives communication and information management throughout the stakeholder network.

A crisis is a challenging time for the organization and its staff. To lead in these instances the manager must engage in five specific activities. Stanley Goodman's work in turning around trouble organizations is a good resource when addressing these challenges.[1] For example, first among the manager's task is to keep the pace of achievement high. This includes achievements in the containment effort as well as regular, ongoing operations. Second, stay involved and keep in touch with the turnaround team. Containment teams are responsible for their work in the containment effort but there are limits to their authority. Goodman's third point is that the organization's leadership must demonstrate support and confidence when things are <u>not</u> going well in the turnaround effort. Addressing a crisis may be a first for many in the containment effort so there are likely to be errors or mistakes. These are mentoring opportunities for the organization's leadership. The organization's leadership knows the range of competencies defining operations so when an error occurs the leader may pull others from inside the organization as one-time resources and problem solvers. Fourth, encourage members of the team with support and recognition of their achievements. And, fifth, Goodman stresses that the manager must work with the turnaround team as a partner, not some distant boss or organizer. This is an underlying theme behind this chapter and the book overall.

For some in management positions these are unfamiliar activities. After all, it was miscues or lack of involvement on management's part that contributed to the mismanagement of the original event or incident so now, in the midst of the crisis, not only do approaches to the crisis have to change, but it also may be necessary to involve different people in the change effort. This last point is particularly important to review. The emergence of a crisis, catastrophe or disaster means that things have and will change in the organization and that something must be done to rectify the situation. The organization's management must take a leadership role in this change effort or, in some instances, step out of the way and let someone else take charge of the crisis and its effects.

This is a common occurrence. The CEO of a hospital does not lead the fire fighting effort when that crisis emerges; that leader steps aside and lets those with the skills, competence and experience handle that crisis management role. Dealing with the crisis remains a change effort, but those leading the effort may not have a direct role in planning and managing activities associated with, in this case, putting out the fire. The organization's leadership is engaged as the overall leader of the effort and the person who owns the overall success of the containment effort.

Containing the Crisis Begins with Understanding the Nature of a Crisis

Table 3.1 in Chapter 3 outlined representative activities when responding to an event, crises, catastrophes and disasters. The key premise behind that sketch is that when mismanagement of an event occurs, immediate action must be taken to prevent the triggering of a crisis that, if mismanaged, can morph into a catastrophe. At the same time, it is very important to recognize that each of these phenomena has the potential to spawn other events, incidents or issues to manage. Overall, the entire effort is a very complicated process, but it is manageable given the right planning and commitment to execution—this is the initial challenge leaders must face and meet.

The material in Table 3.1 provides a useful guide when building a plan to contain the crisis and to manage its ancillary effects. The emergence of a crisis and, if they occur, a catastrophe and disaster, are the worst case scenarios for those in leadership or other key organizational roles. In these instances, those investigating the crisis stream are in a knowledge-needy state; they want facts regarding what happened and why and, if relevant, who is responsible. This also is a significant period for those involved because in addition to damages associated with the crisis, there is the potential for those involved to be impacted as well.

Some societies are making it harder for those in leadership positions to hide behind the "corporate veil" or a well-positioned legal team. So even if some may save their jobs or positions after mismanagement of an event or crisis they should keep in mind that their own personal brand or image as professionals are also at stake. In these instances, the organization's leadership would be prudent to recognize that when stakeholders evaluate the organization, they separate damages to the organization or people from faults or behaviors of those in leadership positions. In these instances, damages to one's personal brand can linger long after the effects of a crisis on the organization fade.

Crisis Containment Preliminaries

Given this brief introduction, those seeking to build a strategy for containing a crisis and subsequent plans for managing crisis effects should keep five important features in mind to be best prepared. First, even though it seems obvious it remains important to note that, *all crises are different*. A fire is different from a flood, from a disease, from threats by angry people, etc. This means that there are some crises your organization may attempt to contain and there are others beyond the skills and competencies of your staff. These are crises delegated to other organizations. In addition, even when your organization is familiar or experienced with a particular type of crisis, that does not mean the staff are prepared. Some may be new to your organization and even those with more experience may not have seen issues needing to be addressed for a long time or within your organization. It also possible that some staff may not be physically able to participate in a crisis containment effort; perhaps they are ill or are suffering from an injury of their own. And, of course, your staff may be fully involved in managing the daily requirements of their own jobs so there is little if any bandwidth to take on additional tasks or activities. An organization should accept responsibility for managing an event when it is clear that the organization's staff have the capabilities and resources for successful management of the event. Let common sense, not vanity drive a decision to address a troublesome event.

Next, *threats associated with a crisis can impact ANY organization and in many different ways*. Think of the disgruntled individual who shows up at a gas station, grocery store or office building, has an argument, and pulls out a gun. Those types of events (the arguments) may happen anywhere but the act of (pulling out a gun) does not. Crises are not predictable. True, organizations in flood and tornado zones should have plans for these types of events, but the crises triggered because of event mismanagement are not predictable, even for well-prepared organizations.

Sometimes the type of organization or the state the organization is in determines how dangerous a crisis' effects may be. Patients within a hospital may have limited mobility, or underlying health conditions that may require physical support systems (e.g., oxygen or wheelchairs). If these support sytems or tools are not available or are difficult to use during, for example, a fire or other crisis then this has to be addressed, particularly when an evacuation is required. Hospitals, nursing homes and eldercare communities also are 24-hour operations, but that does not mean all of its core medical and health staff also are immediately available on a 24-hour basis, however. Contingency plans should be prepared in advance for critical situations that occur in off hours or on weekends. Also, when you think of organizations, it is important to recognize that every large organization is comprised of many different and smaller organizations. These are vulnerable to crises as well and, too, reflect different levels of readiness.

Related to the material just covered, it is important to remember that some organizations have "extended" or transient populations also vulnerable in a crisis. Patients have visitors, different departments have vendors and almost all healthcare organizations have emergency medical teams, healthcare professionals and representatives from different organizations (e.g., social workers) who float in and out of the organization. Their presence can create serious problems in the midst of a crisis. Visitors may want to help, but they also may not know established procedures or even key exit points. Good-natured friends also may not know what the patient needs in an evacuation, particularly when linked to life support or other devices. Visitors may range from the very young to elderly. Their intentions are notable but their involvement in crisis-related activities should be avoided.

A last feature to keep in mind, when defining a strategy for containing a crisis and the plan for managing effects associated with the crisis, is that a *crisis' threats vary with the nature of the crisis*. For example, some effects associated with a crisis may be completely unexpected. Injuries incurred because of a physical attack may be unexpected and if the injuries are to both patients and staff, we are dealing with two different matters. Questions regarding who is treated first may be an issue as well as who is dealing with the aggressor while treatments are administered.

Sometimes the fire crisis that is out of control may seem like a threat to address, but if gas lines rupture and an explosion results, this can have more significant ramifications than just the fire. Or, too, imagine that the explosion hasn't occurred so that people have to operate around the possibility that one may occur. This is a different matter for consideration. People will alter their behavior in anticipation of what _might_ occur.

Clearly, life-threatening crises are of obvious concern, but in many instances, it is not the life-threatening crisis, per se, that is the issue, but rather matters leading up to the maturing crisis. Flames from a raging fire are one factor, but smoke and hazardous fumes associated with the fire are a very different matter. These ancillary conditions may be harmful, as well as unexpected, because they can carry both immediate threats and harm, but also because they can interfere with the overall remediation process underway.

Some crises create unexpected logistical matters for those involved. A fire may mean evacuations must occur, so some people using hallways and entry/exit points are traveling in one direction while those seeking to provide assistance may be traveling in the other direction and, loaded down with equipment meant for crisis containment. In addition, consider what is happening outside the facility during this fire. The media and family members or neighbors may be flooding into driveways and the areas around the building while fire trucks and ambulances are trying to move into the area. What is the traffic management plan in these instances?

Then there are the events that are beyond virtually everyone's experience. One of the benefits of the Coronavirus pandemic is that we quickly learned how little we knew about the virus and how to approach it. Some healthcare facilities wanted to move their infected residents out, while other hospitals and care centers attempted to use nursing homes and eldercare communities as overflow areas for their COVID-positive patients. In addition, those managing the nursing homes and eldercare communities had to figure out what to do with their residents. Should they be restricted to some parts of their facilities or all parts? How are meals handled? Safeguarding healthy residents means protecting them from sick patients so how is that handled. And what about protective gear and clothing—to say nothing about trying to test staff and residents for the virus. These were unexpected details and yet key part of initial crisis containment efforts.

When a crisis occurs, it is possible to expect people to be upset and afraid, but in some instances, fears and panic may dominate entire populations. Some people may fear for their own safety at the expense of others. Other times, the fear turns to despair for this already vulnerable population and the effects can be long lasting. Truly these are extreme cases but given what we have witnessed with matters surrounding the COVID-19 crisis, these are realistic. We often expect there to be physical effects associated with a crisis but the sheer range of emotional and cognitive effects may be completely unexpected even for the seasoned professional.

Finally, a truly traumatized group of survivors may remain when a crisis results in severe injury or the death of one's neighbors or friends. It is sometimes difficult to remember that the patients in a hospital or residents of nursing homes and eldercare communities experience both healthcare and lifestyle changes with their move to these locations. Moreover, since these changes are difficult for some new residents to manage, organizations work to help these individuals build "new" lives for themselves with new friends and new relationships. Now, at this perilous time in their lives, those friends and acquaintances are lost, leaving yet another consequence for the individuals and communities to manage.

The Elements of Crisis Containment: The Strategy and Plan

Aspects of the containment process are reviewed at different times throughout this book. For now, there are two primary facts to keep in mind when building containment plans and strategies. First, the unique nature of the crisis requires that the plan is tailored to it and there is no attempt to pass off some off-the-shelf canned approach as the plan to use. Second, the containment strategy must focus first on overall containment of the crisis with the management of secondary matters spawned by the crisis addressed as related but separate matters.

Regarding the first point, recall that the model used here suggests the mismanagement of an event or incident triggers the crisis and that the crisis that emerges may be significantly different from the event associated with it. Management of events like falls, cuts or scrapes or incidents of diarrhea or even food poisoning if not treated, or are mismanaged, may result in infections, permanent disabilities or other damages. Whatever the case, a different type of response and level of resources (e.g., people, processes, materials and equipment) may be required to manage these more serious situations.

The nature of the incident defines the action(s) to take. This makes sense and if you are working in a healthcare facility then it is likely the staff has some experience with the issues or resources needed to manage the event. But, as the material in Chapter 5's appendix suggests, today's healthcare facility is exposed to more than medical risks and incidents. Cyber-attacks, HAZMAT challenges brought about because of hazardous chemicals or materials, and even incidents of workplace violence are not beyond the exposures those in today's organizations face whatever their line of business. The issue for organizations facing these types of threatening events is that some action is required to contain or minimize risks until external resources arrive.

The best steps to contain a crisis are specific to the nature of the crisis. However, the staff in many healthcare facilities may not have experience dealing with a cyber-attack on their computer system or extreme workplace violence. To address these and other potential vulnerabilities a two-part approach may be useful for dealing with these and other incidents like those outlined in the Appendix for Chapter 5. Table 6.1 outlines how a response plan that matches an organization's resources may be built as a pre-emptive approach to event management. This material defines staff as assistants to professionals brought in to manage events beyond their capabilities. This is an important process because it recognizes that when responding to a serious crisis, even if the organization's staff does not have skills to directly manage an event they may be able to facilitate and support the efforts of those actually containing the crisis situation.

Table 6.1 Thinking preemptively: preparing for troublesome events when the organization's staff are "Assisting Resources"

1.	Identify major gaps in the staff's knowledge given what is needed
2.	If possible identify steps to address knowledge gaps
3.	Assemble professional resources to address knowledge gaps ● Corporate office personnel (e.g., Legal, Management) ● Law enforcement personnel, first responders ● Corporate finance ● Facilities personnel
4.	Define an Incidence Response plan for different types of events ● Define Organizational staff who will be involved as support personnel ● Define the Range of support staff will provide ● Define the limits of support staff will provide ● Identify the Policies, Procedures and Support Plans that must be in place
5.	Disseminate findings to involved stakeholders ● Get stakeholders to review findings with recommendations
6.	Build a Response Plan
7.	Communicate the Plan to Staff, key Stakeholders
8.	Launch the Incidence Response Plan

Leadership, Management and Steps in Defining the Crisis Containment Effort

There is a difference between management and leadership and the following quote by Philip Kotter clearly illustrates the differences. "Management is a set of processes that can keep a complicated system of people and technology running smoothly. The most important aspects of management include planning, budgeting, organizing, staffing, controlling, and problem solving. Leadership is a set of processes that creates organizations in the first place or adapts them to significantly changing circumstances. Leadership defines what the future should look like, aligns people with that vision, and inspires them to make it happen despite the obstacles."[2]

Kotter's distinction between management and leadership is an excellent way to begin the conclusion for this chapter and the book. Troublesome events occur, some are large, most are small, but all need successful management. Failure to successfully manage even the smallest event, we believe, can trigger a more dangerous, dynamic crisis for an organization and its stakeholders. Managers and staff may be dealing with the details, but the organization's leadership owns responsibility for the overall effort.

Material in Table 6.1 illustrates ways to begin organizational activities in a pre-emptive manner. It is a useful guide because it provides a view of tasks associated with preparing for a crisis containment effort. This type of activity is appropriate for different types of incidents listed in Chapter 5's Appendix. Specifics for the organization plan for a crisis containment effort can evolve from the material covered in Table 6.1. But remember, any containment effort has to be defined in terms of the specific crisis. Particulars are everything!

The material that follows serves two purposes. On one level the material provides a way of thinking about the basics, the types of matters that need addressing when preparing a crisis containment effort. On another level, however, each of the steps or points can be viewed as a means for understanding where your organization is in the transition from event to crisis. Sometimes the trigger points, the breaking points that launch a crisis are evident. For example, in medical cases when characteristics associated with what began as a troublesome event spring into what is a life-threatening event. It is a classical "you know it when you see it" type of phenomenon.

Too often, however, the migration from an event to a crisis is more subtle. For example, the event may communicate tendrils of turmoil, some large some not, that move through the organization or the stakeholder social network or the system as a whole. These "tendrils" are like micro events, each with its own profile and schema. This is one reason data collection is such a vital objective early in the event treatment program. Members of the organization need to be sensitive to warning signs that may only be obvious to them given their training or position within the organization. In these moments, every one engaged becomes a leader in their own right. They do not pass off as insignificant something they believe may become "a big deal." Remember, we have described the transition between the event and crisis as a morphing or transformation from one state, the event, into another state, the crisis. Indeed, while the material is presented in a sequential order, this is not meant to imply building a plan of action is some linear process. Sure, it makes sense that some things are done early with others that follow but, in fact, something can and perhaps should be done on all of these "items" without any sense of order. Just do them and make them fit to build your plan.

Steps in Preparing a Plan of Action

Nine items outline this guide for a "Plan of Action." These can be addressed in order as outlined or, again given the challenges you are facing, your staffs' competencies and/or your own experience the steps can be approached as guides and with a sense that some steps are always open for more information as time passes. You might, for example, begin with gathering key data and then move to another item, for example like having an early communication session with stakeholders. The key point is to do something on all of these steps as quickly as possible.

The material that follows focuses on a "physical" crisis, such as a fire or maybe even a disease outbreak. However, it is obvious that all organizations can experience other types of crises such as workplace violence, discrimination or some type of public relations blunder. The materials contained in these nine steps are guidelines and not prescriptions for action. The organization's leadership working in conjunction with its advisors and department management constructs the plan to follow in the containment effort. All of this may be more appropriate to you and your work if, as you read the material, you think of a crisis you have experienced or read about and plug it in as your own example. Make this material as personal to you as possible.

Item one—Profile the Crisis. At this point, the crisis is emerging and it is important to gather as much preliminary information as possible. Describe the "who, what, where, when, why and how" of the crisis. It may not be possible to provide precise material; it is just a sketch for others to build on as they get their information collected.

Additional descriptive information adds perspective by portraying ways the crisis-state is manifesting itself within the environment. Document, or be prepared to document any reports prepared by any who have witnessed the crisis. Prepare communications and formats for reports. Define the make-up of the organization's team, characteristics that may prove essential in this containment effort. Identify important team leader characteristics. Provide suggestions for training the team might need. (For example, negotiation or presentation skills). Stipulate any equipment or materials for the team (e.g., protective clothing).

Item two—Detection and Classification. What activities or behaviors seem associated with the crisis? Think of people associated with the crisis. What types of behaviors are those closest to the crisis displaying? What about those in areas not near the crisis? How are behaviors changing over time? What appears to be significant psychological, cognitive or emotional stress points? Are people fearful, are they traumatized by what is occurring? Have some people displayed avoidance strategies, attempting to get away from the organization until the crisis subsides?

Are staff members near the crisis demonstrating skill deficiencies? Are some individuals standing out because of their technical or leadership skills? Are there enough people in vital areas? Where are their staffing shortfalls or deficiencies?

Item three—Communication with External Stakeholders. Create a Crisis Communication Team with a designated spokesperson. Next, identify those who receive communications, what they will receive and why. List the name and roles of those in the organization and of those outside the organization receiving communications. All of those involved must be told what is public and what is confidential information. Then, those receiving the information must be committed to maintaining confidentiality and silence regarding the crisis. The organization's communication spokesperson manages all communications.

Item four—Levels One and Two for Crisis Containment. Level One is short-term containment. The objective here is to isolate the area(s) where the crisis is emerging and is susceptible to containment efforts. This creates two points in time. The first is where the organization is now; it is a quick patch, a quick fix to define a perimeter for the project team and those effected by the crisis. The second, Level Two, is where full containment is achieved. It is not possible to predict when Level Two containment occurs. In anticipation, however, define any back-up systems or operations that can be used until Level Two containment occurs and regular operations are restored. Level Two Containment is not where the crisis is resolved, it is where damages, outcomes and consequences are restricted or confined. Speculating on Level One and Level Two containment is a first timeline; it only covers the very early moments of the crisis event.

Item five—First Acts to Secure the Crisis Areas. Evaluations and movement of those impacted by the crisis occur. Areas where the crisis impact is evident are cleared and prepared for professional responders. Communication and transportation, if needed, are critical objectives. Create "safe zone" for evacuees. This area should be away from containment activities but accessible to emergency vehicles needed to service the injured.

Item six—Explication of Effects. This is an ongoing activity. Here identify the products, outcomes and impacts associated with the crisis. This analysis examines and reports on key segments of the organization, people and departments. Among the factors covered are people (e.g., staff and their morale, the competencies, strengths and short comings they have vis a vis the crisis, effects on patients, stakeholders, etc.), material (e.g., availability of protective gear), equipment (e.g., like fire extinguishers needed to contain a fire) or processes (e.g., related to safety or security procedures). Immediately pass this information on to support services stakeholders as they arrive.

Item seven—Containment. The crisis is contained. All affected people are receiving the assistance or aid they need. All affected areas (including equipment, materials and processes) are secure. Operations related to the affected area(s) are re-established, pending any needed repairs. Documentation of the containment effort is prepared and distributed to those with a need to know. The organization's leadership approves communication regarding the crisis, with information then disseminated by the communication spokesperson. Describe monitoring efforts used to ensure the restored operations function as expected. Documentation of any resulting changes or enhancements to operations is essential. What tests or evaluations will be conducted to ensure operations function as desired and within the parameters of rules and regulations related to the business?

Item eight—Management of Residual Effects. The emergence of a crisis can trigger ancillary or residual effects to address. Documentation of the triggered or residual effects is prepared also with suggested management plans for them. A timeline is prepared for the management of each effect. What remedies are in place? Which staff are assigned to participate in these efforts?

Item nine—Conclusions, Improvements and Revitalization. Operations return to normal. Document the time to this point, costs incurred, losses, damages or injuries (with the status of each). Detail changes to the organization as a result of the crisis, its effects and any remediation efforts.

Remember, these nine steps are guidelines and not prescriptions for action. The organization's leadership working in conjunction with its advisors and department management construct the plan to follow in the containment effort. And one last important point to keep in mind—sometimes, given the nature of the crisis, containment may take weeks or months to achieve. Be prepared for whatever it takes.

Management, Leadership and a Communication Process

An organizational crisis is an impersonal, change force. A crisis in an organization can shift ways people behave, disrupt operations, break processes and, in the worst cases, lead to a loss of life as well as long-term physical, emotional or psychological damage to stakeholders throughout the organization's social network. Never ignore a crisis but, at the same time, do not attempt to address a crisis the way someone might attempt to manage a troublesome event or incident. The two are very different phenomena. A crisis' destabilizing nature must be contained and effects or residuals defined and managed. This is a two-part process with the first aimed at both containing the crisis and supporting the stakeholder network as defined above, while the second targets specifics; the spin-off incidents and events spawned by the crisis.

The leadership element to accomplish these challenges breaks across two groups: one is the organization's leadership, and the other is the organization's governance segment, the corporate board, directors or advisors. Leadership's role in crisis management follows the path outlined above by Kotter and reflects two primary activities: communicate and change. Communication efforts flow throughout the organization and its social network. These communications keep the organization's governance informed, and those in the social network prepared for and involved in the crisis containment effort. Changing direction implies more than just moving from a problematic point in the organization's experience; it implies moving to a new and better state that is marked by both the end of the crisis as well as a point where learnings from the experience are embraced and woven into the organization's cultural fabric.

An authority in crisis communications, Jonathan Bernstein,[3] summarized the particulars crisis communications may cover and, as such, is a valuable addition to this discussion. Communications associated with the emergence and containment of a crisis in a healthcare environment must reflect the particular nature of those organizations and their social networks.

The first planning step associated with crisis containment communications begins with the construction of a crisis communication team. This idea was touched on above but the important distinction to make here is that the organization's leadership, probably working in conjunction with key department leaders, picks the team, but *does not manage the team or its activities*. The team, through its team leader, works with the organization's leadership to define members in the new social network that has formed because of the crisis[4] and prepares communications to the leadership for approvals before dissemination.

Once the team is in place, planning associated with crisis containment communications begins and ideally before the crisis emerges. This is accomplished in a number of ways, but we recommend by building off the material discussed above in Chapter 5's Appendix. There the discussion focuses on fundamentals associated with communication around an event but takes this material a little farther and asks, "how might this material be used should an event be mismanaged and morph into a crisis?" That type of analysis and forethought can breed a sense of urgency regarding the events as issues to manage, and as a way for preventing a crisis from materializing.

As well as analyzing the nature of the event the team also focuses on ways the organization's social network is changing because of the event. Remember the social network is composed of the original internal and external stakeholders associated with the organization but with the event and/or crisis additional stakeholders will join the network.[5] These new stakeholders can be emergency services, contractors, regulators, the media and litigators (working for you or their clients). Once defined, the communication team works with this expanded network, again working with the organization's leadership, to identify the types of information needed by different stakeholders. For example, know which stakeholders may get full information while others only receive generic messages tailored to their needs as established by the organization's leadership.

A third step is to identify and train key spokespersons in the organization. These are professionals who display knowledge and understanding of the organization and the crisis, and who have the capability to communicate in small or large group settings. Anyone who speaks on organization's behalf must model the organization and its values in addition to having the competencies to manage information. The organization's leadership must recognize the importance of the role of the spokespersons. This is not an assignment for just anyone; it is a critical position for someone whose skills, demeanor and competence reflect an image of professionalism that stands out in a crisis. This person is a leader in her/his own right.

Fourth, everyone associated with communication activities, whether part of a particular team (e.g., the communication team), department management or the organization's leadership must be skilled communicators. This is not limited to situations where an individual is asked to stand before a group and offer thoughts regarding the crisis, but it also includes skills needed to communicate in one-on-one settings (e.g., when working with outside professionals or one's staff) as well as in group and meeting management. Treat these as the important communication settings they are.

During these meetings and information sessions transparency is a convenient buzzword for people to use when describing their objectives, but a crisis containment effort needs more than buzzwords. An organization's leadership must create and maintain multiple communication channels throughout the containment effort; these actions are more than staged transparencies. These channels link with stakeholders and are conduits for both the organization's messages and stakeholder feedback and assessments. Moreover, use of the channels becomes another means for observers to note progress throughout the change effort.

Fifth, one of the most important communications produced during the containment effort is a "holding statement." According to Ward Hubble[6] the holding statement "consists of the few brief sentences you give to the media when they first call immediately after the crisis has occurred. You may not have all the information you need about the crisis to provide a full statement, but you know you need to buy yourself some time as you gather information."

According to Hubble, "Your holding statement should convey to the public, 'We're on it.'" It lets your stakeholders know that "you've done what you can to stop doing harm and contributing to the crisis, and – most importantly – be human. You want to provide the public with reassurance about the situation and ensure them of your compassion, while letting them know of future action." We expand Hubble's notion here to suggest that there also be a holding statement made particularly for the internal stakeholders. It can convey the same message as that prepared for public consumption but, in particularly trying times, it can also convey reassurances and a sense that the containment is a collaborative effort for all. In short, it could be very similar to the media statement while including information more directly relevant to each internal stakeholder's concerns, e.g., how the crisis or changes related to the containment effort impacts our internal daily life.

Sixth, continuously monitor and evaluate the crisis. Much of the power of evaluation is in its contribution to reducing uncertainty, an important need when a crisis emerges. Define data and information pulled together in terms of the stakeholders involved. For example, who needs what type of information and when do they need it. Classify these types of data and update the material on a regular basis or as needed given the requirements of particular stakeholders. It also is important to know who is responsible for collecting the needed data. Some information will come from the organization's staff involved in the containment effort while other information will only come from experts involved in the crisis. Regardless of the source, the communication team routes the information to the organization's leadership and other stakeholders according to the communication plan.

The overarching principle to remember given all the above is that communications during the crisis must reflect that the organization's leadership is involved, personally and systematically, in all aspects of the crisis containment effort. The organization's leadership demonstrates its involvement through all communications and particularly communications designed to summarize key points or events in the containment effort. These may not always be accounts of spectacular achievements or last steps in the containment effort, but whenever released they must honestly report on the status at a given point—good or not. Readers of these communications should come away with an understanding of what happened and why, of what was done and why and, of what remains to be done and why.

The Organization's Leadership and Managers as Change Agents

One of the best ways to characterize a crisis containment effort is as a change process. The objective is to recognize that a new status quo will define the organization. The crisis shapes operations into an unacceptable state. The crisis must be contained, and at the same time, the organization must define a new state, based on what has occurred, learned and, needed for the future. It is not change for the sake of change, nor is this an opportunity to "go back to the way things were."

The organization's leadership directs this change effort, and commitment to it, through a variety of activities and behaviors beginning with a vision for the future: an image of the organization and its operations with the crisis contained. As the crisis is contained and its effects addressed and managed, the rebuilding of affected areas, processes or procedures reflects what we want to see. This is a desire to bring the affected state(s) back as new, functioning operations. Building begins by documenting the rationale for the new vision. How will operations improve, how will service, safety, security, productivity and quality improve and, how will stakeholder needs be better met?

This is a systemic effort, so all members of the new stakeholder network need to be identified and involved. For example, in many instances, once the crisis is contained, any external stakeholders like regulators, fire or police services simply leave. Now, while they are available and the crisis is fresh in their minds, solicit their thoughts regarding improvements or needed change. They have free knowledge and experience to give and, in addition, involving them in the change effort is one way to demonstrate commitment that your organization is not going back to the way it was.

Thinking systemically about the internal and external members of the network affords an opportunity to improve processes throughout the network's supply chain. Members of the network are part of a large provider universe. This multi-functional operation exists because every member of the network contributes to and hopes to benefit from membership. For example, consider an estimate of the "dexterity quotient" between key stakeholders and for the system as a whole. For example, if the nursing department has a one-week supply of masks and gloves and the supplier can fulfill their needs in two weeks then the dexterity quotient is .5 (1 week divided by 2 weeks). That is unacceptable. However, if the vendor can get the supplies to the nurses in less than a week, say in half the time, the quotient (1 week divided by .5) is now 2.0 or 2 to 3 days, and so forth. The point is that network's supply chain is a dynamic sub-system that may have multiple areas to improve. (By the way, the network is a two-way process. For example, the illustration using the masks and gloves supplier goes both ways. We know when the nurses expect to receive the masks and gloves but if the supplier expects payment within 30 days and receives payment in 45 days, that quotient is .66. The closer the quotient is to 1.0 the better and, of course, anything greater than 1.0 is even better. For the supplier this is an example resulting in a quotient of .66 is unacceptable performance.)

Performance measurement provides an opportunity to track how well individual stakeholders/departments work but collecting data has other benefits. For example, data collection is a good way for continuously evaluating achievements, too. Some evaluations measure achievement in targeted areas while others measure improvements or gains in the overall containment effort. Finally, as members in the network become familiar with measurement activities associated with the crisis containment effort, they can learn to incorporate performance assessment into their own ongoing operations after the crisis is contained.

Measurements and evaluations provide numerous benefits. For example, what do you know about your staff's attitudes, beliefs, opinions and behaviors regarding the organization's vision and mission or goals and objectives? As pointed out earlier in the book, consensus around these features are "musts" for the organization's membership. An organization's leadership should be on the lookout for opportunities to improvement performance or to change tired processes but to do both it is important to have valid and reliable information. To see why this is important statement try this exercise. At some time, perhaps in a meeting with department managers, ask each one to write down their idea of what the organization's vision is now—then compare the results. You may be surprised at the differences regarding what should be a central, driving theme for everyone.

An organization's vision should be a simple statement providing operational guidelines for a period of three to five years. There is only one vision and it is the leadership's responsibility to see that staff and operations work in ways to achieve that vision. In this effort, the organization's leader may be a guide, a mentor, evaluator and communicator throughout the network. In this capacity, the leader challenges the existing culture, is unwavering when seeking improvements and is a model of personal change in the process. In some instances, this means improving one's own professional make-up along with everyone else. But the bottom line is that everyone has to be of the same mindset in the pursuit of the organization's vision.

This is engaged leadership. Difficult issues are not avoided. If people are "too busy" to meet, call them on it. If someone regularly cancels meetings or appointments recognize this as the performance issue it is. (They somehow find time to take their vacations!) Look for warning signs, for example, people who agree but do not commit, those who do not share critical information, who rely on "the way we used to do it." Remember, document everything.

Of course, the leadership will display steadfast commitment to the change effort, but do not expect everyone to follow. In addition to stakeholders not able to see your vision, some people may not know how to build something new from what was. Many stakeholders have learned to behave or to work as they do; it is comfortable for them and they may lack the motivation, or are unable to see the need to change. In these instances, they have to stop what they have always done in the past. Others may simply be overwhelmed; the scope and scale of change they are experiencing is too much for them. Remember, they not only have to change in their work area and the way they do things, they have to mesh their change efforts with others who also have to change the ways they are doing things. Patience leadership is the rule in these situations.

Know, too, that just because you have a vision regarding new ways to do things, that does not mean others can share that vision. They may not want to share it, they may not be able to see it or, they may not understand it and, of course, it may not be the best for the organization. For example, if they still have unanswered questions or the vision simply does not make sense they may find it hard to buy into the vision. Whatever the case, it is the leadership's responsibility to see these problems and to provide the clarity and information needed.

Finally, ethical displays say as much about the leadership as it does the organization's culture. It is nice to have friends in the organization, but friends do not receive exceptions. It is one thing to try to protect the organization, but not if what happens in the organization is illegal or harmful. It is important for the organization's leadership to keep in mind that their positions are always in the spotlight. Leadership must portray an image of what is expected for everyone, no exclusions or exceptions.

Leadership by the Organization's Governance: Corporate Board, Directors or Advisors and Change

One thing particularly unique about organizations is that there always seems to be someone higher up in management chain—even for stakeholders at the highest levels! The relationship between an organization's leadership and it board, directors or advisors can be particularly unique. Sometimes the advisory group is a collection of supporters, as those who will rubber-stamp the leadership's wishes. Other times the board keeps the leadership team at arm's length, seeing themselves as representatives of the investors or other stakeholders. However, when a crisis emerges the governance group needs to examine its own role and responsibilities as well as its relationship with the leadership.

A crisis triggers change throughout the organization's social network, including those in the organization's governance circles. During a crisis, information, knowledge, facts and perspective are "musts" for those involved. Moreover, with some crises, there may be a real need to break away from typical approaches to problems and to introduce radical rethinking of one's role. For advisory groups this "rethinking" seems to surface in different ways.

For some the process begins with introspection—the advisory group imagining how it will function and behave during a potentially tumultuous period. Stuart Spencer, an international leadership consulting group partnered with INSEAD, a private non-profit international university and surveyed 2,000 board members and produced a document focused on "what makes a board successful in dealing with such a crisis as Covid-19" authored by Richard Bertrand, 2020.[7] Several themes stand out as pertinent for those in leadership positions in healthcare industry. Among the most notable are the following:

- Permanently challenging crisis management processes can be achieved by thinking the unthinkable and using scenario analysis rather than only relying on existing processes.

- Test the board's behavior in terms of its ability to work under stress and deteriorated working conditions, e.g.:

1. Focusing on the immediate issues without getting lost in details.
2. Staying unified and ensuring overall consistency between decisions made for the short term and the long term.
3. Working efficiently with management to ensure an adequate and clean division of responsibilities between the two bodies without the board overloading management with unrealistic demands that slow down decision processes.
4. Getting used to working remotely with secure communication channels.
5. Celebrating management's successes.
6. Reimagining the future.

- Having clear leadership at the board level which means the chair playing his or her role fully, but only that role.
- Establishing adequate communication within the board and between the board and management, the external communication of the company remaining a management duty.
- Providing emotional support to both management and employees. Performance assessment will come later—a crisis is not the right time to change the CEO.
- Making sure that in dealing with the crisis, management decisions remain aligned with the company's values.[8]

Any one of these responses would be a good starting point for the board reviewing its approach to its advisory role, but taken together they provide a solid and in-depth foundation for a good retrospective review at anytime. A second point to consider when examining a board or advisory group's role during a crisis can be grounded in actions the board or advisory group takes with the organization's leadership or stakeholders in general. Seymour Burchman and Blair Jones,[9] Managing Directors at Semler Brossy Consulting Group, point out that corporate boards "have a fiduciary responsibility to manage risk, especially against major events that could overwhelm an organization and devastate shareholders' investments. The Covid-19 pandemic has forced new attention on board's responsibilities."

The ultimate concern, however, is that organizations are likely to suffer a variety of significantly different crises in the future. "Boards" they write, "have several ways to promote resilience and watch for potential [crises]. They can encourage stress tests in comprehensive risk reviews. They can press management on the worst-case scenarios for each [crisis], including when the threat becomes existential for the company. They can then suggest "war games" to develop principles for effective responses—with lessons brought back to the board for assessment and discussion."[10] In short, Burchman and Jones seek to retool the thinking of board members so that they meet future challenges new and innovative methods.

Lynn S. Paine[11] writing in the *Harvard Business Review* echoed a similar view. Paine wrote that boards are facing a new reality because of Covid-19. "The new environment is characterized by an increasingly complex set of pressures and demands from various stakeholder groups, heightened expectations for societal engagement and corporate citizenship, and radical uncertainty about the future. These factors are complicating board decision-making and challenging the shareholder-centric model of governance that has guided boards and business leaders for the past several decades."

Paine's and the others cited demonstrate that any major crisis does not merely target those on the front lines of change, but that the need for change responses ripples throughout the organization's stakeholder network. And, moreover, those in governance and advisory roles must not only re-examine their own functions but also the functions of those whom they influence and affect. Toward this end, Paine made the following powerful point that we strongly support:

> Shareholder primacy is the cornerstone of the agency-based model of governance, but if the pandemic has shown anything, it is the importance of each and every stakeholder group to a company's ability to function, let alone thrive and succeed over time. In the face of Covid-19, some companies struggled because their customers disappeared. Others saw their workforce reduced to a skeleton crew of essential employees.

Still others grappled with supply chain disruptions, unsustainable debt, or insufficient capital to fund their operations. Since the onset of the crisis, it has become common practice for management to update the board on the situation regarding each stakeholder group, and many boards and senior leaders have declared the health and safety of employees and customers to be their top priority. Some investor groups as well have weighed in on behalf of putting employees first during this perilous time.[12]

Paine's comments point to a third direction governance and advisory groups can take in a crisis, to develop a specific posture that is purposely crisis-related. For example, Paine offers a sketch as to what this crisis-related posture might look like:

These lessons from Covid-19 imply a more active role for boards in monitoring companies' relationships with their core stakeholders. That may mean asking management to continue the Covid-19-born practice of periodic reporting to the board on the status of each group or, more formally, to establish goals and a reporting process that will allow the board to track the company's performance for its stakeholders more systematically over time. Boards will also want to take a more active role in ensuring that tradeoffs among the interests of its various stakeholders are handled in a way that is consistent with its obligations to these groups and with the long-term health of the company. For that, it will be important for directors to have a shared understanding of the company's purpose and strategy, as well as a framework defining the company's stakeholders and responsibilities to each.[13]

Others are even more specific in their recommendations to boards and other governance groups. Dambisa Moyo[14] in another *Harvard Business Review* article highlights a fourth area of concern related to the role of these groups as a crisis breaks. His treatment of the subject makes it clear that a crisis can force a new relationship between the advisory groups and management.

"Management teams and their boards are juggling a wide array of concerns right now [during the COVID-19 crisis], from the health of their workforces to volatile equity markets to shuttered debt markets. Furthermore, many economists and policy makers have slashed GDP forecasts and now portend a deep global recession. So, what should boards do in a moment of crisis such as this?"[15] His answer to that question is specific; he offers ten focal areas for management and boards to use as discussion points during a crisis. Moyo's entire article regarding this discussion is must reading, but for now here are summaries of his ten points paraphrased given the book's theme:

1. **What can you do to ensure the health and safety of your workforce?** This means employees have valid and reliable information regarding the crisis. Collect and report data regarding worker injuries or fatalities.
2. **What is your CEO succession plan?** Every organization needs a succession plan to use in response to the loss of key employees but such a plan is especially important when a crisis potentially threatens the capacity of an employee to work.
3. **What is the company's ability to cover near-term expenses?** Without any history of a specific crisis or in dealing with a crisis, those in leadership positions may not consider the effect of the crisis's lifespan on the organization's resources. So, what is the plan to cover unanticipated expenses over unpredictable time spans?
4. **What tradeoffs do we have to make around payroll expenses?** Here again is an important question to consider. Which are the "must" jobs or positions that the organization needs to function? How are other matters like laundry, meals, housekeeping going to be handled and by whom? Regular staff, contractors?
5. **Do we need to adjust our supply chains?** The impact of the crisis on the organization's supply chain for hosptital, nursing and eldercare communities can vary significantly with the type of crisis or a crisis' length. A crisis that causes a temporary disruption of services is one thing, but a crisis like COVID-19 can affect several aspects of a supply chain's operation. Various types of vendors and vendor behavior can be affected when COVID-19 makes wearing masks mandatory. Even issues like building access can affect supply chain operations. Deliveries are affected if a "lock down" is in effect and it's not possible to make deliveries to the buildings where they are

needed. So, what are the alternatives, and how are these and other changes communicated to the board or advisory group?

6. **Are we prepared to work remotely for an extended period of time?** This is a unique question for those working in the healthcare industry. What happens to communication patterns and expectations when some in administrative roles are working from home while those in healthcare delivery positions are in the healthcare center? Do decision making and leadership patterns change so that communication needs are met without having to wait for a response for someone who is not on site?

7. **How do we keep our company culture alive?** How do we keep the aspects of our company's culture that we want to keep alive, and how do we manage those aspects of a new and emerging culture that form because of the crisis? Both of the dimensions reflect matters of particular interest to the organization's advisory groups. What is their feeling about changes to the existing culture and new aspects of the culture that may be emerging? Clearly this is a significant issue because the organization's culture not only affects stakeholders, it plays a critical role in defining the organization's brand and operations.

8. **How are we interacting with the financial markets?** This question will affect organizations differently. Those that are large financial entities with investors across different functions will be pressed to provide specifics regarding the organization short- and long-term financial profiles. But even smaller operations have concerns here. Disruptions in service affect the organization's debt service, the capacity to borrow may be affected for both the borrower, the healthcare center, and the lender whose operation's may be impacted by the same crisis, as is the case with COVID-19. Numerous stakeholders will have questions regarding associated matters.

9. **How strong is our underlying business model?** Crises typically are not part of the organization business model. For example, COVID-19 dramatically impacted business operations of hospitals and other healthcare operations. Parts of some businesses were closed as the virus flooded emergency rooms and filled hospital beds. Others, like dental offices and support services closed operations altogether. But

COVID-19 does not stand out as the exceptional crisis. Consider a natural event, like a tornado, hurricane or flood where services are denied or staffing cannot access the facilities, what then? Real time data needs to be prepared and relayed to the board when these types of events occur.

10. **Are we behaving as a socially responsible organization?** This may be one of the "questions of the day" for all organizations but its significance is not lost during a crisis. In fact, it is often the case that throughout an organization's experience with a crisis' life span the question is asked many times, so the organization's advisory groups are sure to want answers as well. This also is the type of question that can be asked in terms of stakeholders (e.g., regarding the ways they are being treated), the organization's relationship with the community (e.g., is the organization "a good citizen"?) and, of course, in the treatment of residents.[16]

Finally, Jeffrey Sonnenfeld[17] in his article, "What Makes Great Boards Great" highlighted a particularly interesting advisory group/leadership issue when he noted that it is

> difficult to tease out the factors that make one group of people an effective team and another, equally talented group of people a dysfunctional one; well-functioning, successful teams usually have chemistry that can't be quantified. They seem to get into a virtuous cycle in which one good quality builds on another. Team members develop mutual respect; because they respect one another, they develop trust; because they trust one another, they share difficult information; because they all have the same, reasonably complete information, they can challenge one another's conclusions coherently; because a spirited give-and-take becomes the norm, they learn to adjust their own interpretations in response to intelligent questions.

Now what makes Sonnefeld's observation salient for our discussion is that the *relationships* that need to be great are not just those intra-group relationships in a particular healthcare organization. The advisory groups within the entire systemic stakeholder network also must communicate

and work together for the sake of the system as a whole! This is particularly true for that period during a crisis but it also true when there is
no crisis and routine, day-to-day matters define the organization and its
operations within the network.

It often appears that trying times brings out the best and worst in
people, at all levels of the organization. If an organization, for whatever
reason, feels better than, more deserving than or more important than
others in its social network, this is a problem—for itself and the network
as a whole. Trying to ferret out who is most important, most special, etc.
is hardly the thing to do when in the grips of a crisis.

Conclusion

In the face of a troublesome event or emerging crisis people often ask,
"Who 'owns' the event management or crisis containment effort?" or
"Where does the "buck stop?" Our answer to both questions is that
ownership for these efforts rests with the organization's executives and,
importantly, also with the organization's Board and advisors. What we
expect to see at the top of today's healthcare organizations is "change
leadership." Leadership that embraces change, innovation, and discovery
as the foundation for action at any time, whenever it is needed.

This last point is easy to say and is a quick theme to rally around,
but in the midst of a crisis, it hardly seems like something one wants to
have to say. Embracing change in a crisis can be dangerous because as we
have pointed out, change permeates a crisis. Everything about a crisis is
change. Some like to talk about a new normal but again, what is normal
during a crisis except change, and change is not normal for most people
or organizations.

Next, what about innovation? Opportunities for innovation in a crisis
seem to pop up everywhere. The problem is that things are happening
so fast, who notices the innovation or has time to think about them?
Some innovations are acts of desperation, just to get something done
in the spur of the moment. Sure, ideally, it would be nice to sit back
at the end of the day and think through the day's events and note the

innovations that occurred but, at the end of the day, who has the energy and, too, who has been taught to care?

Lastly, what about that "foundation for action?" In a crisis one of the major issues facing those in the crisis is that there are few set rules for *any* action. Sometimes the rule is "get away with whatever you can get away with!" Here, again, the issue is that change is driving action in a crisis so the response to change-driven action is, simply, some other, ideally, counter-action. There is no foundation, per se. There may not even be boundaries, there is just action.

So, this conclusion's opening paragraph, drawn from the first page of this chapter seems, at best foolish, and at least hard to treat as realistic. Yet, and this is the underlying point behind the chapter: this paragraph is valid and, if for no other reason, it demonstrates why and how lack of preparedness that can trigger a crisis is so costly.

If while reading this chapter you thought of any of the crises in the day's news and you wondered "why are these things happening?" "They don't make any sense!" then you are beginning to see the potential value of material covered in this chapter and the book as a whole. Just look at the news tonight and look at the monies lost, the time lost, the lives lost all because of peoples' mismanagement of events. If you aren't getting the education you need on crisis containment from this book, then get it yourself by asking questions about the world around you. Then do something else!

Notes

1. Goodman, Stanley J. *How to Manage a Turnaround: A Senior Manager's Blueprint for Turning an Ailing Business into a Winner*. New York: The Free Press, 1982, pp. 238–9.
2. Kotter, John P. *Leading Change*. Boston: Harvard Business School Press, 1996, pp. 25–26.
3. Bernstein, Jonathan. "The 10 Steps of Crisis Communications" on the website, https://www.bernsteincrisismanagement.com/the-10-steps-of-crisis-communications/.
4. Tafoya, Dennis. *Organizations in the Face of Crisis: Managing the Brand and Stakeholders*. New York, NY: Palgrave Macmillan, 2013, p. 49.

5. Ibid.
6. Hubble, Ward. "The Art of the Holding Statement," March 13, 2018, https://www.thinkhubbell.com/art-holding-statement/.
7. Bertand, Richard. "The Effects of Covid-19 on Boards and Governance." Stuartspencer.com. October, 2020.
8. Ibid.
9. Burchman, Seymour and Blair Jones. "How Boards Can Prepare for Unplanned Catastrophic Events." Harvard Law School Forum on Corporate Governance, September 19, 2020, *HBR.com.*
10. Ibid.
11. Paine, Lynn S. "Covid-19 Is Rewriting the Rules of Corporate Governance." *Harvard Business Review*, October 6, 2020, HBR.com.
12. Ibid.
13. Ibid.
14. Moyo, Dambisa. "10 Questions to Guide Boards Through the Pandemic." *Harvard Business Review*, April 10, 2020, https://hbr.org/2020/04/10-questions-to-guide-boards-through-the-pandemic.
15. Ibid.
16. Ibid.
17. Sonnenfeld, Jeffrey. "What Makes Great Boards Great." *Harvard Business Review*, September 2002, https://hbr.org/2002/09/what-makes-great-boards-great.

7

Marshalling the Change Needed for Crisis Containment and the Post-crisis Period

Abstract Two objectives capture the change needed to manage a troublesome event or to contain a crisis. The first objective is that plans are prepared that lay out a means for addressing the challenges brought on by the event or crisis. The second objective is that the plans and efforts associated with designing and executing management or containment efforts must build trust in the new, post-event, post-crisis organization. A crisis that materializes because of an event's mismanagement undermines not only the organization's operations but also the brand or image for the organization and its leadership. This new state can cause stakeholders to wonder if the organization will be able to fulfill its obligations to meet their needs and if the organization's leadership is trusted to capably lead the organization.

Keywords Containment and leadership · Performance vs accountabilities · Risk and crises over time · Alignment vs misalignment · Reputations and trust at risk · Influence and persuasion · Resistance to change

© The Author(s), under exclusive license to Springer Nature Switzerland AG 2021
D. W. Tafoya and L. Poeth, *Healthcare Leadership in Times of Crisis*, https://doi.org/10.1007/978-3-030-75965-0_7

Two objectives capture the change needed to manage a troublesome event or to contain a crisis. The first objective is that plans produced lay out a means for addressing the challenges brought on by the event or crisis. This means plans must be systematic in their orientation to the stakeholders, processes, procedures, materials and equipment needed to change the organization. It also means that planned change efforts should embrace any need for change in the organization's culture and leadership. The second objective is that the plans and efforts associated with designing and executing management or containment efforts must earn and build trust in the new, post-event, post-crisis organization. A crisis that materializes because of an event's mismanagement undermines not only the organization's operations, but also the brand or image, and its leadership. This new state can cause stakeholders to wonder if the organization will be able to fulfill its obligations to meet their needs and if the organization's leadership can be trusted to capably lead the organization. This is a point in a crisis when levels of potentially destabilizing uncertainties surface.

Everything About Containment Centers Around Leadership

The management of events can involve any one in an organization. In a hospital, the initial managers might be part of the emergency response team transporting an individual to the emergency department or the admission's personnel processing a walk-in. From those entry points the individual passes from professional to professional, each with an opportunity to manage the event that presents itself. And this is an important point, for while a specific health emergency might have initiated the event for the EMT or admission's staff, the character of the event for the patient changes as time passes and as each new staff member comes in contact with the patient.

A number of different events affect this patient in our example, with each managed by individuals in a number of different roles, any one of which may trigger pre-conditions for a crisis if the event is mismanaged. Moreover, the nature of the events can vary in size and complexity.

A "needle stick" is a small event, but the crisis it can trigger might be a life-threatening experience. So, on one level, our interest is in the management of events but, on a very different level, we are interested in performance issues; how well individuals handle their assignments.

These conclusions are true whether we are examining the work of a staff or line employee or members of the healthcare organization's leadership. Yet, examining the management of events or the emergence of a crisis in terms of a healthcare organization's leadership introduces another dimension to this discussion. A healthcare organization is responsible for operations on two fronts: the multitude of events that define any given moment or day, and the leadership requirements specifically linked to an event "going bad" or a crisis.

An organization's leadership has oversight and responsibility for the overall environment. This is true for those at the very top of the organization as well as those responsible for individual departments or divisions. The key idea in that last sentence is responsibility. Leadership of an organization, whatever its size or nature, translates into responsibility for that organization, for a project or at the smallest levels, a task. So, the leader of an organization may transfer part of the overall responsibility for a project, like the management of an event or containment of a crisis to one or more individuals. However, the overall responsibility for the success of the management or containment effort remains with the organization's leadership; the organization's leadership shares both the successes and failures associated with work done by subordinates.

Initial responsibilities come with the nature of one's position, while at other times someone in an organization's leadership stream may delegate additional responsibilities in the form of assignments or tasks. At no time, however, does anyone completely relinquish the responsibilities associated with their span of control. Delegation of responsibilities does not release the leadership from responsibilities for a project or task assigned to another.

Containment Requires Leadership on Two Fronts

When a crisis emerges, its containment becomes the responsibility of the organization's leadership. This is an added responsibility to the leadership's existing responsibilities, to one's particular position and span of control. For example, when an accountant creates an error leading to a "financial crisis" for the organization, the organization's Chief Financial Officer assumes part of the responsibility for that crisis and the error triggering it. Those in leadership positions are responsible for their own work and for any work done by those in direct or indirect reporting relationships, sometimes referred to as their chain of command.

Measuring levels of responsibility associated with management of an event or crisis containment is not always a straightforward process. Most important is that evaluation criteria need to be prepared and agreed upon. Then, using core performance criteria, different tools and measures, match these to the type of crisis. Among the typical basis for measurement criteria in this instance are criteria associated with people, processes, materials, equipment, time and the organization's culture. Finally, it is best to use a combination of qualitative and quantitative indices to track the distribution of responsibility. This provides a means for understanding who has responsibility for different tasks or projects, and when and where efforts related to crisis containment succeed or fail.

Table 7.1 illustrates one way to track accountabilities across different organizational levels, from top management through staff positions. Notice that while each of the three staffing levels has "job specific" levels of accountability, the leadership has 100% responsibility for all operations and activities. There are several other important things to note regarding responsibilities in the table. First, in any organization, if you sum up all amounts of responsibility the total is 100%. The percent may vary from job to job but there is never more than or less than 100% in an organization. Even if someone calls in sick, for example, the need to have that person's work covered means someone else has to accept (or be assigned to) those responsibilities until the person returns to work. For example, think of an admissions staff person in a hospital. If one of the admissions staff calls out sick, patients still need to be admitted,

Table 7.1 Tracking performance against accountabilities

	The Organization's Leadership Responsibilities & Accountabilities Overall: 100% Job Specific: 35%		
Organization's: Vision & Mission Planning & Finance	The Organization's: Policies & Practices Strategies & Tactics	The Organization's: Stakeholder Network Performance Expectations	The Organization's: Budgets & Resources Materials & Facilities
	The Organization's Management Responsibilities & Accountabilities: Job Specific: 50%		
Operational: Performance Planning Operational Goals Reporting	Operational: Staffing & Evaluation	Operational: Staff Management	Operational: Project Management Evaluation Reporting
	The Organization's Employee Base Responsibilities & Accountabilities: Job Specific: 15%		
Daily: Task Performance	Daily: Collaboration	Daily: Quality, Productivity Safety, Security	Daily: Project Performance
	Performance against Expectations for the organization as a whole: Variable		
Performance toward: Vision & Mission Goals & Objectives Operations	Performance by: Divisions Departments	Performance by: Area Operations	Performance by: Special Projects Emergency Projects

so someone else has to accept the responsibilities for the person who is absent.

Second, amounts of accountability may shift as conditions change within an organization. For example, if someone falls in the hospital (a troublesome event), those nearby may stop what they are doing and shift their responsibilities to help this person. The assumption here is that the shifting of responsibilities is a lateral move, that is, helping the person who fell is within the span of control of the person offering assistance. If, on the other hand, someone with a gun enters the hospital and shoots someone, the person shot needs attention that may be beyond those nearby, so the responsibility for care is delayed until someone capable is available. There is some responsibility to getting the help that is needed, but that is not the same as administering aid.

Finally, note that the manner in which the terms "responsibilities" and "accountabilities" are used defines a closed system with each person's tasks defined in terms of certain accountabilities. Some of these accountabilities are pro forma; individuals are accountable for the work done. Other accountabilities link to specific tasks, like preparing reports or conducting evaluations with the completion of work or assignments. Regardless of the nature of these accountabilities, each is a form of communication that can flow back up the organization to various managers and leaders. They are part of the organization's information processes.

The two conclusions to draw from this discussion is that at no time can an organization's leadership (including advisory or corporate boards) deny a role in organizational efforts to manage events or contain a crisis. It is all too easy to pass off challenging issues or problems to those at operational levels of an organization. After all, they are the ones "doing the work". But, the ultimate catalysts that enable and empower those who do the work come from the decisions about that work made at the leadership and management levels.

Containment Must Envision Both Immediate and Long-Term Impacts

Apart from its physical features, a crisis is a dynamic pool of energy.[1] In and of itself, the crisis per se does not cause problems or damage people or property. The problems or damages, the "causes" associated with a crisis, stem from an array of products, outcomes and impacts surrounding the crisis. Combined, they are both effects of the crisis, and the crisis itself.

This is not an exercise in semantics. COVID-19 is an event. A crisis emerges when the virus spreads (a product) because people do not wear masks or practice social distancing and hospital emergency rooms become over crowded (an outcome), and healthcare providers become sick, hospital rooms are full and people die (all of which are impacts). This line of reasoning was presented earlier, and it is reintroduced here because threats to organization result if the crisis is not contained, and those threats are "risk".

Diagram 7.1 maps the relationship between risk over time as a crisis continues in an uncontained manner. The risk line follows the evolution from the mismanaged event and the resulting impacts as a linear relationship, but that is not valid assumption. In fact, because a given crisis can trigger numerous products and those in turn, numerous outcomes, and those numerous impacts, the emergence of risk does not follow a linear pattern. In short, a given crisis can trigger disorder and create risk, as confusion and chaos emerge in a number of different ways at a number of different times.

Some of these risky effects may be predictable while others are not. For example, consider the effects spawned by COVID-19's mismanagement. There was an inadequate supply of staff clothing, respirators or other equipment. Initially, there were no known remedies or treatment strategies. There soon became limited hospital space in emergency rooms and on other floors. Operating budgets were not prepared to cover costs associated with the virus and its products, outcomes and impacts. COVID-19 arrival in the United States was an event, waiting to be managed.

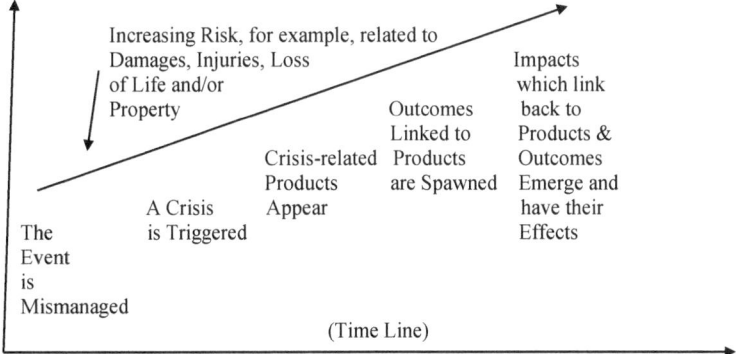

Diagram 7.1 Illustrating the relationship between risk and features of a crisis

And if all of this was not bad enough, what the above paragraph describes is just one stream associated with the initial products. The levels of complexity associated with a crisis should be mapped over short-term and long-term periods. The latter, for example in the case of COVID-19 to cover the lack of available vaccines, relapses, trauma due to stress and the ever-present likelihood that the virus would morph into completely new strains.

If we revisit the discussion regarding "responsibilities" above, now we can see that an emerging crisis is not just "that thing in front of those enlisted to contain it" but rather a multifaceted, dynamic system that potentially touches every member of a stakeholder network over near- and long-term periods. The emergence of a crisis can send shockwaves through the organization's stakeholder network with each new product triggering significant risk exposures. If the organization's management is competent and the organization's architecture, operations and brand are sound, then the crisis' effects may be controlled. However, if any of these areas are weak, poorly defined and the organization's overall system is out of alignment, the dangers associated with the emerging crisis increase, as does overall risk exposure.

Earlier in the book, material outlining role and importance of organizational alignment to performance stressed the importance of this critical feature and pointed out that recognizing the value of this concept *after* a crisis emerges is far too late. So how does your organization measure up in terms of alignment among key operational areas or features? An article by Jonathan Trevor and Barry Varcoe[2] provides valuable insights into how organizations become "misaligned" in the first place. Together they identify four reasons why many organizations "go off the rails" because of misalignment. Here is a summary of the reasons they list.

First, they write, some organizational leaders "are unaware of the risks of misalignment." "Many senior executives we talk to do not think of their enterprises as connected and coherent value chains. Their primary focus is all too often on their enterprise's structure as articulated by the org chart. The main operating units described there are seen as being the primary components of 'value.' Alignment thinking requires *all* decision makers to view their enterprise as a value chain, not merely a set of more or less valuable boxes and wires on an easy-to-forget, ever-changing chart."

This last sentence is especially important for those thinking about the effects of a crisis on the organization. Alignment, operations and the organization's brand link to become the organization as we know it. This linking is critically important, but it also is why pressures or effects associated with a crisis may appear to affect one area but, in fact, are transmitted among the three. This transmission is one way chaos in the midst of a crisis complicates the spawning of effects and containment efforts. Looking to contain a crisis means simultaneously thinking, looking and acting systemically.

A second reason Trevor and Varcoe note is that "nobody 'owns' enterprise alignment."

> Generally, no individual or group is functionally responsible for overseeing the arrangement of the enterprise from end to end. Multiple individuals and groups are responsible for different components of the enterprise value chain, and usually they are not as joined up as they should be. All too often individual leaders seek to protect and optimize their own domains and components, rather than align and improve across the entire enterprise.

This conclusion regarding ownership of an organization's alignment parallels a similar point regarding crisis containment efforts. They write that while few in organizations know who is responsible for ensuring the organization is aligned the answer "cannot be 'nobody' or "I don't know.' Neither can the answer be 'the CEO' (or equivalent). Modern enterprises are too complex for their design and management to be left to chance or to rely solely on the wisdom of one individual."

The same is true during crisis containment efforts. The CEO's accountabilities and responsibilities stream through the containment efforts but actual containment is realized *throughout the organization*, whether the crisis' effects were localized or not. For example, assume that a crisis occurs in the Emergency Department, where it also is subsequently contained. Now, think about the other stakeholders who are directly or indirectly effected by this crisis. If the department is shut down, then EMTs seeking to drop off new cases may be delayed or diverted. The crisis affects patient care through delays as the department attempts to resume operations. The finance department may have an unanticipated expense and insurance exposures and, some departments are responsible for repairing damages and securing the ED for operations. This is just a summary of other stakeholder departments impacted. What about effects on people, like the caregivers (the doctors and nurses, social workers) other those in other support areas like those managing traffic, food services or maintenance? In the end, everyone owns a part of the containment effort regardless of his or her proximity to the actual event.

A third factor Trevor and Varcoe see associated with organizational misalignments is the *complexity associated with today's organizations*. It is easy to get lulled into a workaday world where performance benchmarks are meetings held or reports reviewed. These types of activities may define one's day, but they certainly are not representative of the organization's scope and scale.

> "Achieving and sustaining high enterprise alignment is hard," they write, "especially in a rapidly changing operating environment. Complexity usually arises as the result of four primary factors: number of employees, variety of business lines, variety and expectations of differing customer groups, and geographical dispersal. Large, diversified, and geographically dispersed enterprises, in whichever sectors they compete, require the greatest amount of strategic effort by their leadership to be aligned."

Trevor and Varcoe make a good point here but, in many instances, it reflects only part of the reason misalignments occur because of today's organizational environments. Added to complexity is the role "complications" contribute to misalignment. David Benjamin and David Komlos[3] believe humans are very good at linear thinking, but that complex problems cannot be solved with a linear approach.

> "Here's the thing" they write, humans "can master highly sophisticated technical and technological challenges because we're very skilled at making linear connections from one technical feat to the next. But when it comes to multi-dimensional challenges, it's a whole different ballgame. We can't solve them with linear thinking or rely on technical prowess. Sometimes, they move and change at a rate faster than we can act. They

don't patiently await solutions. They are complex problems–which is a whole different ball game than merely complicated issues."[4]

Given the material presented earlier in Table 4.2, ensuring and/or fixing alignment issues in organizations defined by so many different factors is a complex problem. Benjamin and Komlos note that the "most significant challenges leaders face today are complex in nature. They are issues like doubling the growth of a business, transforming a culture, offering a world-beating consumer experience, complying with new legislation, or stemming an epidemic. The problem is that leaders try to solve these highly complex challenges as if they were merely complicated, and that's a problem." We would of course add to this that managing a troublesome event or emerging crisis also presents complex challenges to those attempting to address these phenomena. The nature of the challenges brought on by crises, catastrophes and disasters are magnified if the organization is out of alignment when special complications associated with the crisis and its effects multiply in the organization.

Returning to Trevor and Varcoe's work, a fourth factor they identify that contributes to misalignment is leadership and management mistaking activity for progress. "The frantic activity of business as usual can get in the way of the in-depth discussions and tough choices that need to take place regularly to lead a strategically aligned enterprise (and maintain it). Ensuring that the whole of the enterprise is as aligned as possible *should* be business as usual for enterprise leaders." Once again, we see the value of staying on top of an event to prevent a crisis from emerging, and staying in front of crisis containment efforts when there is a threat at hand.

Some in organizations seem to criticize the organization's leadership for being "too detail oriented" or for "getting into the organizational weeds" of the day-to-day operations. There is some value in this complaint. Leaders need to be aware of operations, but it cannot consume them or their work; they must let their managers manage. The emergence of troublesome events or emerging crises creates different situations with different levels of organizational risks associated with them. These need the full (or at least fuller) attention of the organization's leadership.

To maximize organizational performance and particularly when managing events or containing a crisis, the organization's leadership must complete two tasks. First, define what successful alignment looks like for the organization during these times and second, devise the means for observing, assessing and ensuring alignment exists as designed and with the benefits expected. Neither are insignificant tasks.

There is no single path to follow that leads to these two objectives, so the organization's leadership should look to, and involve, both internal and external stakeholder networks in this effort. Then, working with this lineup, the leadership should build a problem-solving team of experts that both a monitor of the organization's alignment and act as a strike force when misalignments occur.

Also, as a last thought for the organization's leadership in this effort, that strike force needs to recognize it has the primary responsibility in this effort to be both monitors and change agents. Change requires many resources but most importantly, it takes leadership with vision beyond short-term results. Failure to lead in this instance may result in greater problems associated with unsustainable performance and an uncertain future.

Crises are unpredictable, they are dynamic and diffused energy sources; they create and spread chaos and, more often than not, their nature can be truly new to those expected to contain them. Herein lays the next containment challenge: containment is a knowledge and information drain for the organization's stakeholders.

Containment Is Knowledge and Information Dependent

Events typically do not occur in or near the organization's executive suites. Events affecting the organization or its stakeholders occur in off-site locations, in production centers and sometimes in facilities not even part of the organization's formal operations. As a result, the amount of *real* information needed to contain a crisis may be limited or incomplete. Consider, for example, if you were at a zero-point as far as information is concerned. This is not a position most leaders like to admit that they are in but, frankly, admitting it when beginning a containment effort might be the prudent thing to do. After all, most others involved are likely to recognize the absence of information or knowledge as a real time fact, so why not describe it as such.

Recognizing what you know and do not know is a good position from which to seek involvement of others. For example, if the crisis is related to technical matters, what experts can you call on as resources? What resources do you have available if there are potential legal issues or a need to communicate with the media? These resources may not only help in the containment effort, they are bridges when building interactions with others. This last point is important because in a crisis' earliest stages it is not possible to forecast the full range of damage or injury possible, so better to have key resources useful in dealing with truly dangerous crises so they can collect and process information along with you.

Ultimately, your interest is in getting involvement and support from wherever you can. As you get information, begin to speculate on containment fixes. Since this is early in the process, let three categories of fixes guide your thinking. First, there are the "musts" that are evident, even in these early stages. Next are fixes that "meet" fundamental needs regarding the containment effort—fixes that are relatively easy to implement. Finally, there are "nice to have" fixes. These are literally downstream parts of the containment effort that may add little value overall but, in the end, may make some stakeholders happy with the final product.

To complete the containment exercise to this point, it is important to get support from key stakeholders, in both internal and external networks. Work with your team to sketch ways the crisis is impacting stakeholders and then back out leaders within the stakeholder net who represent impacted areas. Always be prepared to educate stakeholders, to give them information regarding what you know about the crisis, the people, processes, material, equipment, and cultural aspects that are affected. A prerequisite here is that your efforts should be honest and clear, particularly regarding the costs associated with the crisis. Finally, always be prepared to describe secondary effects associated with the crisis: the physical, emotional, psychological traumas experienced throughout the social networks.

One key source of knowledge and information is provided by adversaries. These people are not likely to be concerned about your best interests, but knowing more about their positions and needs will add to the scope of information you have regarding the overall crisis. In addition, dismissing this segment of your external social network only adds to the sentiments of loss and injury, and one thing you probably do not need when trying to contain a crisis is opposition, along with what you are dealing with on the crisis front.

Finally, avoid overpromising or overstating your progress in the containment effort. Everyone wants to know when the "end" will appear, but too bad. Your goal is to build a crisis containment process defined by honesty and reliability. If you have bad news, pass it along, even if you seem only to be passing along bad news for extended periods. Remember, even if everyone in your audiences believes they can do it better—they probably cannot. Again, this is why gaining knowledge and information throughout the containment process is critical for attaining your objective and capably managing your position.

Containment Puts Reputations and Trust on the Line

Crises tend to reek of influences, good and bad. Even before the crisis emerged, the stakeholder network began to grow as adversaries, malcontents, regulators, special interest groups, the media, and an array of litigators added themselves to the pool of people with whom those in the containment effort must meet. As this happens, it is important to keep in mind that all of them have a right to join the network. They represent people, positions, ideologies associated with the crisis and its effects. Pushing them away or attempting to deny them access only adds to the problematic aspects of what is occurring.

Influence is a measure of pressure, and other pressures are obviously linked to the crisis itself. Early in the book, the range of potential effects associated with a crisis were mapped, but these are the most evident influences or pressures one sees. Imagine standing in front of a flaming fire and seeing the flames and feeling the fire's heat. This is one level of pressure on you at the moment, but should the fire begin to burn your skin or damage your eyes, then you experience a second level of the fire's influence. Finally, there are the subtle, sometime insidious ways this fire can work on your psyche, on your emotional make-up. This type of influence may have particularly long-term effects on you and how you see yourself, to say nothing about how you feel about fire.

This may seem a strange metaphor, but its personal nature is a way for introducing you to the range of pressures others might feel from their experience with a crisis. Keep in mind, that when we talk about a crisis, we are talking about a process, and one facet is that people do not have to be part of the crisis scene to feel the crisis' effects on others as well as on themselves. Influence, in whatever form, is real and has effects.

Our point here is that a lot of thinking goes into building a plan or taking action in the face of a troublesome event or crisis. The irony is, that even with these efforts, all too often events are mismanaged, and a crisis emerges. We have used the recent COVID-19 pandemic to illustrate this point.

A crisis' effects on you, your organization and stakeholders are part of a real-time drama that needs to be contained, and your role in that containment effort is to become an influencer yourself. The model below illustrates ways an influential person can motivate others to join a containment effort. Notice that in the model, as in life, some may never fully join into the efforts to contain the crisis; they just may not see it as "part of their job."

A leader's role in the crisis containment effort is to motivate others to not only do their work, but to work toward the goal defined in the crisis containment plan. This is an important distinction because in doing their work, in using the skills and competencies toward the plan's goal they also are *investing* in the plan's outcome: containment of the crisis. Diagram 7.2[5] illustrates how influence can unfold in a crisis containment effort.

Note, too, that joining into the effort defined by the plan may have little to do with the position one has in the organization or the stakeholder network. Some in management or leadership positions may be

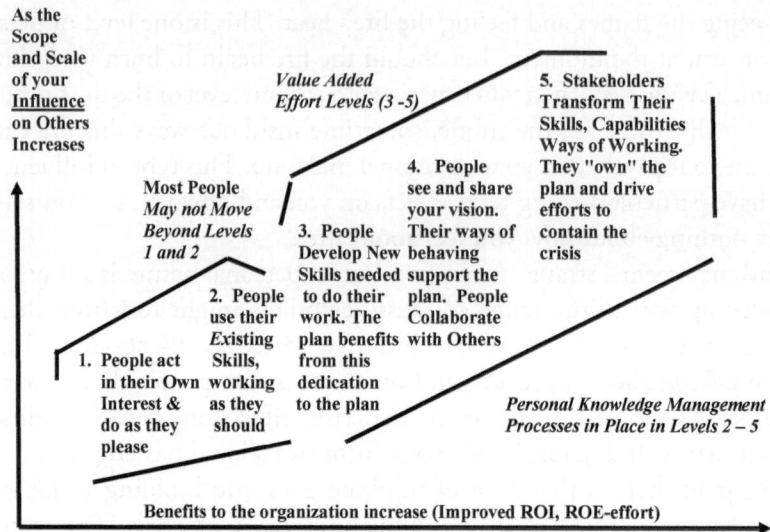

As the
Scope
and Scale
of your
<u>Influence</u>
on Others
Increases

Value Added
Effort Levels (3 -5)

5. Stakeholders
Transform Their
Skills, Capabilities
Ways of Working.
They "own" the
plan and drive
efforts to
contain the
crisis

Most People
May not Move
Beyond Levels
1 and 2

4. People
see and share
your vision.

3. People
Develop New
Skills needed
to do their
work. The
plan benefits
from this
dedication
to the plan

Their ways of
behaving
support the
plan. People
Collaborate
with Others

2. People
use their
Existing
Skills,
working
as they
should

1. People act
in their Own
Interest &
do as they
please

Personal Knowledge Management
Processes in Place in Levels 2 – 5

Benefits to the organization increase (Improved ROI, ROE-effort)

Diagram 7.2 Influence via personal action and competence: Potential "value added pay-offs" demonstrated with the personal action model©

among those at level 2 in the bottom left of the diagram; they do their work as they should but that is all. The motivation to behave in this matter is beyond the project's containment effort at the time but it is a performance issue to address in the future.

Conclusion: There Is a Difference Between Influence and Persuasion

At some point in the containment effort, the organization's leadership will recognize that while change is necessary to contain the crisis, other change will be required for stakeholders as they enter the post-crisis period. Some these changes will require new processes and procedures; some may result in the elimination of positions or perhaps entire departments. New safety, security, quality and productivity requirements may translate into dramatic changes within the stakeholder network.

Influence alone will not bring about these types of changes. Often stakeholders must be persuaded to join in these new ways of doing things and, in some instances, not given a choice to join or not.

Many parallels between and influence and persuasion are obvious. Seeking out and understanding the other's needs, wants and desires is important for both. Being respectful, kind and compassionate are other features to practice as you seek to grow involvement. Now, as containment becomes a reality, it is necessary to look at change from a different perspective.

First, frequently through a containment effort, those in leadership positions have opportunities to scan the mix of activities launched to address the crisis as a way to measure the plan's progress. While taking this opportunity, it also is wise to anticipate the nature of changes that may be required to complete the containment effort and advance the organization into and through a post-crisis period. This introduces a new issue for those in leadership roles: are stakeholders ready for the changes that may be coming their way? Organizations are successful in part because they have developed intelligent, consistent ways of doing things. Now, with the crisis and its aftereffects, it may be necessary to do things differently; to introduce change to prevent another crisis from occurring and/or for simply doing things differently because some changes seem warranted.

Second, as the leadership team begins to speculate on the types of changes that may be required to complete the containment effort or to prepare for the post-crisis period, the leadership must assess the organization's capacity to manage the types of changes anticipated. There are costs associated with any change efforts. There are financial costs, but there also are costs associated with people, processes, material and equipment needs. Process, material and equipment costs are addressed in detail as the need for a change is clarified. People costs are discussed below, but it is important to note that in addition to that discussion, some change may affect the organization's culture and, one way or another, that too becomes another "people cost."

Members of the organization help create the organization's culture but, as stakeholders, they also invest in the culture as part of who they are. In what ways will the organization's culture be affected by proposed changes, and in what ways do stakeholders have to be prepared for those changes? You may see the change as "organizational" but for individuals the change experience is personal. Changes to the organization's culture can impinge on an individual's emotional and psychological make-up. Cultural change can be tricky and should not be taken or approached lightly.

Change in these types of instances may be threatening for a number of reasons. Some will resist change because it is change, so it is important to impress upon everyone the rationale behind the suggested changes. Others will resist change because they may not feel personally or professionally ready to perform in the "new" organization. Managing this type of resistance often means adding yet another level of change that seeks to prepare stakeholders for performance in the new environment. At a minimum, this may simply mean some "retooling" is necessary, in other cases a complete professional re-engineering may be required. Whatever the case, plans, tools and processes should accompany the presentation of these new changes so that stakeholders can see that their needs will be addressed along with the new changes.

Then there are those who will resist change for the sake of being resistant. They may not have bought into the containment plan, they may not see the need for doing things differently or, they may simply not want to work along with the change team. This is a performance issue and must be addressed as such. In these instances, the organization's leadership works with its internal professionals in law and human resources to address these and any other performance issues that arise. The crisis threatened the organization and was contained, now this level of resistance may threaten the post-crisis period, and it too must be contained.

Third, what types of systemic changes will the crisis, the crisis' effects or the containment effort require? Crisis containment efforts require a focus on the immediate needs brought on by the crisis and its effects. Beyond this focus, what broader requirements for security, safety, quality or productivity changes will facilitate the organization's movement beyond this post-crisis period into a proactive future? All too often when a crisis' threats are contained, there is a tendency to revert back to the way things were, back to what was familiar. This should not be allowed to occur.

The opportunities to learn from what was experienced can be significant, so the prudent leader will work with the containment team, stakeholders and others to identify what these opportunities are, rank them in terms of importance, and begin efforts to introduce these changes into the organization. Additionally, earlier change has been addressed in terms of particular individuals. Now it is time to explore how change will impact stakeholder networks as social systems. Throughout the book, internal and external social networks have been a foundation for key discussion points. This makes sense, but it also is important when considering the impact of change on the organization. Examine ways change may ripple through the sub-networks that define these large social networks.

Close examination of the two large networks will reveal ways they are comprised of a variety of smaller sub-networks. Examples include sub-groups of friends, of cliques, or business units. When change is introduced to a social network, all of the issues just discussed above are appropriate, but so are issues regarding ways change may affect these sub-groups. So, at the network-wide level change can target people, processes, materials, equipment, time, finances and other business elements. The impact of change at the sub-group levels may be very different than what was discussed.

Change at a network's sub-group level can threaten culture within the organization itself. People in organizations are more than employees or members of the organization, they also are friends or companions. They may have bonds that transcend the organization because they were created and nurtured in religions, family ties, social clubs or through recreational activities. Regardless of where or how these bonds and sub-groups developed, any change that affects one member can be interpreted as affecting (and threatening) the entire sub-group.

Addressing the need for change among stakeholder networks is a good place to end this overall discussion. Earlier containment efforts were described as time-dependent exercises; efforts that are launched to establish boundaries within which the organization's leadership attends to the crisis. Change, too, is linked to a temporal dimension but the nature of time in this instance may be protracted, with the effects of change lingering long after the crisis is contained. As a result, when a crisis emerges within an organization everything about the crisis immediately becomes part of leadership's legacy. It is part of the job.

Notes

1. Tafoya, Dennis. *Crisis, Catastrophe, and Disaster in Organizations: Managing Threats to Operations, Architectures, Brand and Stakeholders*. NY: Palgrave/Macmillan, 2020.
2. Jonathan and Barry Varcoe. "How Aligned Is Your Organization?" *Harvard Business Review*, February 2017, https://hbr.org/2017/02/how-aligned-is-your-organization.
3. Bejamin, David and David Komlos. "How to Tell if a Problem Is Complex or Merely Complicated." Fastcompany.com. https://www.fastcompany.com/90344944/complex-vs-complicated-problems, May 7, 2019.
4. Ibid.
5. Tafoya, Dennis. *The Effective Organization: Practical Application of Complexity Theory and Organizational Design to Maximize Performance in the Face of Emerging Events*. NY: Routledge, 2010, see p. 99.

Index

© The Editor(s) (if applicable) and The Author(s), under exclusive license to Springer Nature Switzerland AG 2021
D. W. Tafoya and L. Poeth, *Healthcare Leadership in Times of Crisis*, https://doi.org/10.1007/978-3-030-75965-0